33 Percent Rockstar

Music, Heartbreak and the Pursuit of Rock Stardom

S.C. Sterling

Thanks to my family, friends and all the bands I shared a stage with. Special thanks to my amazing girlfriend.

Author's Note

This book is a true story and based on events of my life. The names of some people have been changed, and dialogue has been recreated to my best recollection of those exchanges.

33 Percent Rockstar

Liner Notes

Music was my first love. I was fifteen when I purchased my first CD with money from my first paycheck from my first part-time job, washing dishes at a buffet restaurant. I remember the anticipation I had riding home from Sam Goody in the backseat of my mom's Ford Taurus. The CD was the self-titled studio album released by Temple of the Dog, a supergroup featuring members of alt-rock giants Pearl Jam and Soundgarden.

I arrived home and ran to my bedroom, unwrapping the CD packaging with the excitement of a kid opening presents on Christmas morning. I listened to that album probably five times that night and twenty times over the next few days. I was in love.

I was also mesmerized. The vocals, the guitars, the drums created a sound that I had never heard from my parents' Kenny Rogers and Oak Ridge Boys records that I was subjected to growing up. At that moment, I knew I wanted to play guitar. I knew I *had* to play guitar.

There was just one problem: I had never held a guitar, let alone played one. The closest I had ever come to playing an instrument was shaking a handbell in my sixth-grade music class. My performance was mediocre at best, and it didn't extend beyond that classroom.

I also had zero musical talent and was extremely musically challenged. I didn't know the difference between a hi-hat and crash cymbal, or melody and tempo, or distortion tone and clean tone. Fuck, I didn't even know the difference between an electric guitar and bass guitar.

I was twenty when I purchased my first electric guitar, a white Fender Stratocaster. I never learned how to play that guitar, but I never gave up on music—or the dream. A few years later I bought an Ibanez bass guitar, but this time I stuck with it. After countless hours of practice and persistence, I finally became a musician. Eventually, I'd become a damn good one.

Music has been the catalyst for some of the best and worst moments of my life, and this is my personal account of those moments and my attempt to become a rockstar. I became discouraged at times. I became arrogant at times—and I also became an asshole at times. I wanted to quit playing music on multiple occasions. I never made much money, but it was never about the money. For the majority of this story I lived paycheck to paycheck, paying rent a few days late and constantly worrying about my debit card being declined. There are no cliché stories here. No stories about drug-fueled orgies or driving a car into a swimming pool. And no stories about heroin overdoses or performing sexual acts with a groupie and a freshly caught red snapper.

This book is about the love of music and my life as a musician. It includes my triumphs and struggles, my ups and downs, and it details every significant event during my musical career: the good, the bad, and the ones I would rather forget.

I calculate that I've played over 500 shows in a period spanning almost two decades. Everything from my musical career fits into a storage box that contains CDs, old demo tapes, 8 mm videotapes, various-sized T-shirts, band posters, stickers, and faded pictures. I also have the music, and the memories.

Appetite for Destruction

(Or Chapter 1)

November 2004

The closest I came to rock stardom was on November 2, 2004. As the night began, I stood alone on a sidewalk across the street from a flashing marquee preparing myself to play a show in front of over a thousand people. I was twenty-nine and played bass guitar in a punk band that was opening for the punk band Agent Orange and the horror-punk legends the Misfits at the Gothic Theatre in Englewood, Colorado. In less than six years I had gone from musical incompetent to playing the biggest show of my life, but I still hadn't accomplished everything on my musical checklist.

I had arrived two hours before the doors officially opened, and there was already a line of about a hundred people stretching down the sidewalk beyond a used car dealership. Everyone was dressed in different attire but was essentially wearing the same uniform: punk band T-shirts, leather jackets with sewn-on patches, and Dr. Martens or Converse Chuck Taylor All Stars. The outfits were completed with piercings, tattoos, and hair colors ranging from black to pink to green to purple.

I walked past the crowd carrying my black guitar case covered in stickers from bands like Pennywise, Rise Against, and blink-182 and momentarily stopped and glanced at the main entrance. There was a piece of paper taped to the glass door.

TONIGHT'S SHOW SOLD OUT

I smiled and nodded with approval. Of course, the show wasn't sold-out because of my band, it was the Misfits that accounted for the majority of ticket sales. But my band was the opener and that was an achievement—even if it was a small one.

"Get me into the show, man!" yelled a guy wearing a Black Flag T-shirt with a two-foot-high liberty spike mohawk.

"Sorry, I don't get a guest list tonight," I replied.

He raised his hand and extended his middle finger.

"Have a good night," I said as I turned away and walked towards the alley and the back entrance of the Gothic.

The Gothic Theatre is located at 3263 South Broadway and about a twenty-minute bus ride from the state capitol. It opened in 1925 as a silent movie theater and was renovated into a music venue in the late 1980s. It's a medium-sized venue, and bands like Nirvana, the Beastie Boys, and Rage Against the Machine played there before achieving mainstream success and moving on to larger venues.

I had played the Gothic at least a dozen times in various bands throughout the years, but all of them were small shows consisting mostly of local bands. At those shows I was lucky to play in front of four or five hundred people. On one occasion, I could count almost everyone in my eyesight while playing. There's a certain level of embarrassment in playing in front of fifty people in a venue with a capacity of 1,100.

Tonight's show was different from the local ones where I had to beg people to take free tickets to see me play. It had been sold-out for weeks. It was for a national band, a touring band—a professional band that earned their income from playing music.

4

For this show I had friends calling me to beg and barter for tickets.

I offered all of them the same response: "I'm lucky that they let *me* in."

I walked through the parking lot of the Gothic and approached the back door. I was stopped by a security guard, but after a brief conversation he ushered me into the venue and down the staircase that led to the standing-room only general admission floor section.

I'd always admired the architecture of the Gothic, and it reminded me more of a museum than a music venue. The walls are highlighted by a lively blue and green color scheme that flows from the floor to the vaulted ceiling and featured an elegant chandelier that looked like it had hung there since Prohibition. It felt like a disgrace that in a few hours the bathroom floor would be covered in vomit.

The Misfits were performing soundcheck as I walked onto the floor. It was loud, almost deafening, as the sound bounced off the concrete inside the venue. I considered stuffing my ears with toilet paper to construct do-it-yourself earplugs but opted against it.

Jerry Only, the bassist and lead singer of the Misfits, stood at center stage with his signature devilocks, wearing a black hoodie and black sweat pants. Ramones member Marky Ramone was on drums and Dez Cadena from Black Flag was playing guitar. I was starstruck watching thirty years of punk rock history perform a private soundcheck for me and a few Gothic employees.

Jerry looked like a giant standing on stage. He was only 6'1", but he had an intimidating demeanor and even though he was seventeen years older than me, he probably could have kicked my ass in mere moments. He instructed a sound guy above stage right to adjust monitor levels. This continued until he was satisfied. They then played a song and after each band member gave their approval they exited out of the back door into the alley and onto their tour bus.

I removed my orange Ernie Ball Music Man bass and began the process of tuning the guitar. In the background, bartenders and barbacks were unboxing cases of beer, stocking hard liquor bottles on shelves, and dumping buckets of ice into the ice bin.

The Misfits and the Ramones were punk rock royalty and early pioneers of the genre. They influenced generations of punk, pop-punk, melodic punk, horror punk, hardcore punk, garage punk, emo, and almost every other punk subgenre imaginable. I had seen Misfits and Ramones patches on leather jackets since I went to my first punk rock show, an AFI concert, a decade earlier. The two logos were some of the most recognizable ones in rock and roll history and were printed on T-shirts, patches, jackets, and hoodies across the country and world. The Misfits and the Ramones were on the Mount Rushmore of punk rock, next to the Clash and the Sex Pistols. Playing this show was the equivalent of playing a game of one-on-one with Michael Jordan.

"Hey ho, let's go!" I hummed to myself.

I finished tuning and leaned the bass against the wall. The guitar had numerous dents and scratches and other battle scars from the countless shows I had played with it. The largest blemish was from my attempt to imitate Nirvana's Krist Novoselic's performance at the 1992 MTV Music Awards by tossing my bass into the air and catching it without missing a note. Like Krist, I also failed to perform this feat, and the bass landed on a crash symbol before falling onto the stage, resulting in a half-inch indentation on the second fret of the neck.

Even with the blemishes, it was beautiful. The color, the shape, and the sound it produced were at times breathtaking. I loved that bass, and why not? It had produced better memories than most of my ex-girlfriends. Over the years, I had spent hours upon hours playing it and had even fallen asleep with it in my hands. I never named it though, and always felt guilty about it. It was like not naming the family pet.

I had paid $1,250 for the bass from a Denver Guitar Center, and at the time, it was the second-largest purchase I had ever made. The largest was my second car, a baby blue 1978 Ford Mustang I got while I was still in high school, but that I had to finance.

The rest of my band arrived during Agent Orange's soundcheck, and we patiently waited for them to finish so we could begin our own. They took about an hour, and we finally loaded our equipment onto the stage around 6:25, completing our last soundcheck song at 6:58, two minutes before doors opened.

I pressed the mute button on my amp and leaned my guitar against my Ampeg 8x10 cabinet. Then I jumped off the stage and walked towards the bar.

I sat alone at the bar and watched as the audience trickled in. The crowd was small at first, but within ten minutes it felt like I was surrounded by a hundred people, all of them attempting to get the attention of the bartenders. The sound of countless indiscernible conversations, cans of beer popping open, and shot glasses being slammed down onto the bar top filled the room.

It was close to our set time, and I still had to perform my pre-show exercise routine: which included stretching, jumping jacks, and knee tuck jumps. I started this ritual before the third show I ever played and continued it out of superstition, like I was a baseball player who wouldn't step on the foul line as I came on and off the field. I also wanted to avoid pulling a hamstring in the middle of our set, which would've been embarrassing.

I jumped off my stool and proceeded to the VIP backstage area.

"Where the fuck do you think you're going?" asked a security guard as I approached the backstage doors.

I casually pointed to the backstage sticker affixed to my pants.

"Sorry about that," he responded.

"No problem." It felt good to be a rockstar, even if it was only for a few hours.

I walked through the VIP doors and came to a staircase that led to the backstage area. When I got there, I saw a piece of paper taped to a pole near the entrance to the stage:

7:00: Doors
8:10-8:40: Local Opener
9:00-9:45: Agent Orange
10:00-11:30: The Misfits

I took my phone out and the time displayed 7:55. I slipped the phone back into my pocket, then peaked out from behind the curtain to the concert floor. It was already filling up with people attempting to claim their spot.

I began to feel a sense of urgency. I still had to do my pre-show exercises, use the bathroom, get two bottles of water, and go back to the bar to purchase two beers, because a set time of thirty-minutes always required at minimum, two alcoholic beverages on stage. I released the curtain and started down the stairs.

Backstage at the Gothic wasn't behind the stage but below it, and it could only be reached by the staircase, a treacherous beast that was difficult to maneuver when sober and near impossible with a mid-level buzz. At the bottom of the stairs were two rooms and two bathrooms that were surprisingly clean and well maintained. The total area probably had a maximum capacity of twenty or thirty, but on multiple occasions I had seen somewhere around fifty people crammed into it.

Each room included two second-hand couches that looked like they had been donated and purchased, and then donated and purchased again until they found a final resting spot in the basement. They were worn and saggy and emitted a foul odor of beer and cigarettes. A few unmatched end tables and other various pieces of furniture completed the décor. A refrigerator in one of the rooms usually contained cases of bottled water, cheap beer, half-eaten meat-and-cheese trays, expired condiments, various fruits, and, on special occasions, turkey and ham sandwiches.

I carefully rushed down the stairs and hurried toward the fridge. As I entered the second room I looked to my left and saw Marky Ramone sitting alone on a couch drumming on a practice pad. Marky was fashioning the signature Ramones look: tight jeans, black T-shirt, leather coat, and the Ramones' signature bowl-style haircut.

I walked to the refrigerator, grabbed two bottles of water and shut the door. Marky didn't acknowledge me, he didn't even look up from the practice pad. This was the closest I had ever been to a celebrity and I couldn't think of what to say. I felt like a kid praying to get an autograph from his favorite football player. Nervously, I decided to sit in the chair across from him. I opened a bottle and quietly took a few sips. After a minute or so, I finally spoke.

"How's it going?" I asked.

He slowly glanced up then spoke, "Good, thanks." Then he returned to his drumming exercises.

The gravity of the situation quickly sank in. I was sitting in front of punk rock royalty and asked, "How's it going?" I felt like an asshole. He was probably harassed every day by fans and there he was, sitting alone without anyone bothering him, and I attempted to make small talk. I felt like a *big* asshole. I decided to exit as quickly as I entered.

"Have a good show man."

"Thanks," he said, without looking up.

In the adjacent room I ran in place and did jumping jacks until my heart rate was up and I was almost out of breath. I rested momentarily then ran upstairs, placed the water bottles onto the stage, went to the bar, ordered two beers and carefully maneuvered back through the crowd with a can in each hand. I joined the band on the side of the stage and the five of us patiently waited to play.

Minutes later, the PA music stopped and the house lights dimmed. That was our cue, and we walked onstage. The crowd began to cheer and I got goosebumps throughout my entire body. This was the moment I had always dreamed of.

I picked up my bass guitar, spit onto the stage, pressed the unmute button, and plucked the E string. Then I waited for the drummer to count off with his sticks to begin our first song.

I awoke with a pulsating thump of a massive hangover. Warm sunlight beamed onto my face and I quickly shifted my head in an attempt to hide from the light. I was afraid to open my eyes, knowing that would only increase the hangover intensity.

I was a mess. My mouth was dry with the taste of vomit. My neck felt like I had slept with my head at a right angle, and my right hand was wrapped around my penis. I did a quick, silent prayer that I was in my bed and alone. The last thing I wanted was to be naked with vomit on my face in an unknown bed.

I slowly began to open my left eye and the first thing I saw was a black pillow case. This offered no clue as to my location. I decided to go for broke and opened both eyes as wide as possible, temporarily blinding myself in the process.

Once I recovered my vision, I recognized my belongings: my TV, dresser, nightstand, cell phone, and other meager possessions spread throughout the bedroom. The clothing I wore the previous night was scattered on the floor.

I exhaled in relief. I had made it home and was in my own bed. I always considered that a minor victory. I was a little concerned that my guitar and equipment were nowhere in sight, but I would worry about that later.

I glanced down at my mattress and saw Taco Bell hot sauce packets, shredded cheese, lettuce, and a half-eaten taco on my bed. I was uncertain if I should vomit again or finish the taco for breakfast.

I pulled the bedsheet off to reveal that I was naked except for my boxers around my ankles and one sock on my left foot. I never slept naked. I concluded that I didn't bring a girl home and thus must have passed out mid-masturbation session after attempting to eat Taco Bell.

I was naked and hungover. I was unsure where my equipment was or how I got home. I was also unsure if I did anything stupid or embarrassing, but I had a gut feeling that I did at least one idiotic thing. That was usually the case when I was blackout drunk.

"Fuck, I am pathetic," I said as I crawled out of bed.

There I was, at the pinnacle of my musical career—and passed out alone with a taco in my bed and my penis in my hand. I was so drunk I couldn't even masturbate to completion. My career only went downhill from there.

It's Only Rock and Roll
(Or Chapter 2)

July 1998 – January 1999

I was twenty when I purchased my first guitar, a used white Fender Stratocaster I got from a friend for $400. The purchase nearly depleted my savings account, but I didn't care. I owned a guitar, and not just any guitar—it was a replica of the Fender Jimi Hendrix played at Woodstock. It was beautiful and I considered it a piece of art.

I returned home after the purchase, removed the Stratocaster from its black nylon gig bag and gently rested it on my bed. I stared at it, unsure what to do. I had seen hundreds of concerts and countless guitar players, and they made it look easy. I thought once I was in possession of the guitar I would instinctively know what to do. That didn't happen.

I stared cluelessly at the rosewood neck and six nickel-wound strings. I didn't know how to play, not one single note. I didn't even know how to tune the guitar properly.

I decided to stall and searched the pockets of the gig bag. The small sleeve contained picks of various colors, shapes, and sizes, a couple individually wrapped guitar strings, and a broken strap. I placed the accessories next to the guitar and continued searching the bag. The larger storage compartment contained a guitar tablature book for the Nirvana album *Nevermind*, a discovery that caused me to bounce on the bed like a giddy toddler.

Tablature is an alternative to sheet music. It diagrams finger placement on guitar strings and frets, sans any actual musical notation. It's CliffsNotes for musicians who can't read music, and from my experience, the majority of musicians can't. Tablature was going to be my only chance to "read" any form of music, because I had a better chance of learning Russian than reading and writing music.

I thumbed through the book searching for what I deemed the easiest song in the twelve-track, diamond-certified album. I selected track number three, "Come as You Are."

I made a crease down the book's spine and placed it on my lap. Then I shuffled through the pile of picks, ultimately selecting a red one that I positioned meticulously between my thumb and index finger on my right hand. I picked up the Stratocaster and wrapped my left hand around the neck, sliding it up and down across the frets.

I glanced at the book, then at the guitar, then back at the book. Then back down at the guitar.

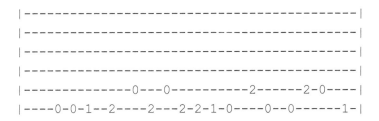

It looked simple enough, but I was completely perplexed. The numbers felt closer to binary code than a song from a trio of Seattle punk rockers.

"Zero, zero, one, two. Zero, zero, one, two," I said as I nodded my head.

I spent the next twenty-minutes attempting to place my fingers on the correct frets with my left hand while simultaneously trying to play the correct strings with my right hand. Nothing.

I took a short break to regroup. I cracked my fingers and neck and performed a few stretches. After a few minutes I attempted the intro again. This time it resulted in a horrible-sounding version of the song, but I could faintly distinguish something that sounded like "Come as You Are."

"I think I'm actually fucking playing this!" I told myself.

I continued playing for the next five hours. A few times I got close to playing the entire intro, but almost every other time it sounded like I was playing an out-of-tune guitar upside down.

The song didn't require any chords, didn't have any complicated rhythms, only utilized the two top strings, and was performed on the first two frets. It was four notes on two strings, but in an entire evening of practice I was barely able to play even the very rudimentary intro. It was frustrating. I decided to take a different approach.

The following day I went to a local music store. I walked directly to the book and magazine section and located the how-to-play-guitar titles. There was an endless inventory of similarly titled books like *Teach Yourself to Play Guitar* and *Guitar for the Absolute Beginner.* After quickly skimming through a few of them, I selected *Beginner's Guide to Electric Guitar* and crammed it under my armpit so no one in the store could see the title. Then I walked to the register.

As I was standing in line I looked down at the cover and became hesitant. I wasn't sure if I should spend $14.99 on a book that featured a middle-aged overweight man with a bad goatee and comb-over who was awkwardly posing with a guitar. He looked more like someone who would sell me an insurance policy than someone who could teach me rock 'n' roll. I didn't have a high degree of confidence in the book, but I decided to go against my better judgment and made the purchase.

I returned home and followed the step-by-step tutorials for the remainder of the day. After attempting to play various sections of different nursery rhymes and "Take Me Home, Country Roads" by John Denver I arrived at two conclusions:

1. Learning how to play the guitar is hard, and it takes a lot of determination and practice.

2. Even if I became obsessed and followed a strict practice regimen, I couldn't be entirely sure if I had any musical talent or ability, and not possessing any talent would be a rather large challenge in learning the instrument.

I glanced down at the book and noticed the recommended age was "5 and Up."

"Fuck you and your recommended age range!" I said as I flung it across my bedroom.

The thought of a first grader being able to play "Mary Had a Little Lamb" more proficiently than me was demoralizing. Unsurprisingly, practice happened less and less. Days turned into weeks into months and the beautiful white Fender Stratocaster found its new home: the back of my closet collecting dust.

After less than six months of ownership, I sold the Fender at a pawn shop for a hundred dollars.

I was sitting next to my friend Jake in my Ford Ranger. We were parked in an empty dirt lot, drinking beers, listening to music, talking music, and playing air guitar and air drums on the steering wheel and dashboard. The parking lot drinking music

15

consisted mostly of nu-metal bands like Korn, Limp Bizkit, and Deftones. My music preferences were still adolescent and naïve. I preferred music that was loud, angry and featured a heavy guitar sound with dropped-D tuning.

I had known Jake since the sixth grade and his passion for music equaled mine, but there was one major difference between us: Jake could actually play an instrument. He was a talented drummer, I'd even go as far as calling him an exceptional one.

Jake started playing the drums in elementary school and continued playing throughout middle school, eventually joining our high school marching band. He played snare drum in the percussion section of the drumline and performed at competitions throughout Colorado and nationally.

The four years of marching band and percussion ensemble classes added to Jake's already-high musical intelligence. He could read and write music and possessed a vast knowledge of music theory and terminology. He was an actual musician—Mozart compared to me.

The first time I saw him play a drum set was at a house party with a bunch of high school bands. All the other bands sounded like shitty high school bands, but Jake's sounded professional, primarily because Jake was such a masterful drummer. He was far and away the best musician at the party. He made drumming look second nature. I could watch him play for hours, hitting the snare, toms, and cymbals with wooden sticks in each hand and bouncing his feet up and down to trigger the bass drum and hi-hat.

For Jake, drumming was an obsession. It seemed like he was always doing something drumming-related: either pounding on a drum set or hitting a practice pad with drumsticks or banging on a steering wheel with his hand or talking about drumming. His life revolved around drums, and at times it was overwhelming.

I was staring out the front window listening to a cover version of George Michael's "Faith" while Jake was drumming fiercely on the dashboard. Suddenly he stopped and looked over at me. He was about to speak but stopped, then started chugging a Pabst Blue Ribbon. He resumed drumming on the dashboard, but with less intensity and volume.

"Why don't you go buy a bass and we'll start jamming?" Jake said.

"Are you fucking joking?"

"No. It would be a lot more fun playing music than staring at dirt and getting drunk while listening to music."

"I completely agree."

"Then what's the problem?"

"I don't know how to play bass and I sold my guitar because I sucked. Fuck, I was absolutely horrible."

"I know you can play. You just didn't give it enough time."

"If you saw me play you wouldn't be saying that."

"Bullshit. I bet I could teach you."

"Do you know how to play guitar?"

"No."

"Have you ever played bass?"

"Not really," he said. He stopped drumming, finished the Pabst Blue Ribbon and crunched the can, dropping it onto the floorboard.

"Won't that be an issue?"

"I don't think so," he said as he opened another beer.

"How do you plan on teaching me bass if you have never really played one?"

"You don't worry about that. I know I can teach you basic music theory, rhythm, some techniques, and scales. And once you get an understanding of those you'll be able to play."

I contemplated his offer. I knew I wasn't talented enough to learn on my own, but if I had an actual musician who was willing to provide lessons in exchange for a constant flow of cheap beer I might have a fighter's chance.

"Do you think you can really teach me?"

"I know indeed."

"This isn't just some bullshit drunk talk is it? Are you 100 percent serious?"

"Yeah," he said as he resumed drumming on the dashboard.

It's widely known in the music community that the bass guitar is the easiest instrument to learn. I'm not saying that all bass players are bad, but for every band that has a talented bass player on the level of Flea, Paul McCartney, or Geddy Lee, there are thousands of bands that feature a bass player who can't keep a steady rhythm. Bass guitar is easy to learn, but hard to master. And though I cared about mastering the instrument, I really just wanted to be decent enough to play a few songs and join a band. I would've been satisfied with average.

"Fuck it, let's give it a try."

A few weeks later I walked into a Guitar Center and made my way to the wall of guitars. The wall stretched at least a hundred feet wide by thirty feet tall, and guitars hung off the wall stacked four high. There were hundreds of guitars, with offerings from Gibson, Fender, PRS, Rickenbacker, Ibanez, ESP, Jackson, Washburn, and Epiphone in almost every color, shape, and style conceivable. The prices attached to each guitar's tuning peg ranged from a few hundred dollars to over $10,000.

I stared at the wall romantically. My idols were all guitar players: Cobain, McCready, Morello, and Gilmour, and I so desperately wanted to play their songs on guitar, but I knew I couldn't. I blamed my genetics that resulted in my fat fingers. I knew if I was going to become a musician, it was going to be as another failed guitar player attempting his hand at the bass.

I slowly turned my back to the wall and walked into the smaller, less-impressive bass guitar room. It was about twenty feet by twenty feet and contained twenty or thirty basses scattered throughout, surrounded by bass cabinets and amplifiers.

I was in the room for a few minutes inspecting the various price tags when a salesman snuck up behind me. "Feel free to jam on any of these guys."

I looked at him, then back to the basses, then back to him. "I've already made up my mind. I'll take that black Ibanez."

I purchased a black four-string Ibanez bass with dual pickups and silver volume and EQ controls for the price of $599. I selected black because it was the opposite of the white Fender, and I hoped my next attempt at becoming a musician resulted in the opposite outcome of my first one.

For the second time in less than a year I depleted my bank account for an instrument I didn't know how to play. I knew the more expensive the purchase, the more motivated I would be to learn, and the last thing I wanted was another guitar that became relegated to the back of my closet or a shelf at a seedy pawnshop.

I arrived home from Guitar Center and removed the bass from the gig bag, attached the strap, and placed the guitar over my shoulder. I walked into the bathroom and stood in front of the mirror staring back at myself. It looked good. It looked natural. Bass guitars are longer than electric guitars and have thicker strings more befitting to my body type and fat fingers.

I plucked the top string, which resulted in a clicking sound. It wasn't much, but it was something. It was a start.

"Are you ready for this?" Jake said.

He was sitting on a chair opposite of me with a rubber drum practice pad in his lap and Promark 5A drumsticks in each hand.

I glanced down at the bass, then to an open notebook on my bed. "I think so."

"I promise if you continuously practice everything I give you, you'll be playing in less than three months."

"Three months?"

"Maybe less than that. I am a pretty amazing teacher."

"I hope you're actually as good of a teacher as you think you are."

"I am. Are you tuned?"

"I think so."

"Well, let's get fucking started!"

He turned on a metronome and set the beats per minute to 60.

Click . . . click . . . click . . . click.

"I want you to pluck the E string on every click. You know what string that is, right?"

"The top one?"

"Bingo."

Click . . . click . . . click . . . click.

He started to strike the practice pad with a drumstick on every click.

Smack . . . smack . . . smack . . . smack.

I watched Jake for a few moments then clumsily shifted my entire upper body in preparation to start playing. I positioned my thumb on top of the pickup and my index finger on the top string.

"Feel the click and just play along with it," Jake said as he continued to hit the pad.

I nodded then began a silent count: one, two, three, four, one, two, three, four, one, two, three, four. I extended my index finger and plucked the E string on the first click. I did it again on the second click but was premature on the third one.

"Fuck, fuck," I said.

"Don't worry about it. You're going to fuck up. You're going to fuck up a lot. You just need to keep playing," Jake said, without looking up from the practice pad.

Click . . . click . . . click . . . click.

I did a quick four count to get back in rhythm with the metronome and resumed playing with the click. I was successful for a solid thirty-second period, not missing even one click. I was so excited I stopped playing.

"Holy fuck, did I just play along with that?"

"Don't fucking stop playing!"

"Sorry, sorry."

We continued this novice exercise for the next few hours, sometimes at a faster tempo, sometimes at a slower one. On rare occasions I played close to perfection, but during most attempts I was off-time or missed playing the string entirely. I wanted to toss the tiny black beeping box onto the floor and stomp on it. It seemed like it should have been a simple exercise, but it wasn't. It took complete focus and concentration.

"It's almost four in the morning and probably a good stopping point for tonight," Jake said, barely able to keep his eyes open.

"I'm good with that," I said. I was on the brink of mental exhaustion.

I glanced down at my fingers. I had become so captivated with the lesson that I didn't realize two dime-sized blisters had developed on the tips of my index and middle fingers on my right hand.

"I don't know how much more I can play anyways," I muttered, flaunting the blisters.

"Those are some nice battle scars. Don't pop them or you won't be able to play for a few days." Jake said as he pushed himself off the chair. "I'll be back here tomorrow at eight."

"Do you think we should take a day or two off to let these heal?"

"I'll see you tomorrow."

For the next three months we practiced at least three nights a week, and occasionally as much as five nights a week, sometimes partaking in two-a-days. Jake taught me the fundamentals: beginning music theory, essential rhythm skills, tempo, intervals, scales, chords and anything else he thought was essential to my training. He was Mickey Goldmill and I was Rocky Balboa.

Some nights we practiced for three hours, and some nights we practiced for six hours. Some nights we drank and practiced, and some nights we practiced and drank. The blisters gradually became calluses and my musical dexterity gradually increased with every session.

"Remember, the intro is boom . . . boom, boom, boom. Boom . . . boom . . . boom, boom. Boom, boom," Jake said, altering his tone with each note.

"Will you please just fucking hit play?"

He pressed play on the cheap Sony CD player and we patiently waited for sound to come from the speakers.

"Three, two, one," Jake said, barely audible while holding his hand above his head and counting with his fingers.

I closed my eyes and started playing. I was forty-five seconds into "Creep" by Radiohead when I realized I was actually playing the song essentially note for note.

I wish I was special, you're so fuckin' special.

"Here comes the chorus!" Jake announced with excitement while drumming with his hands on his thighs to the rhythm of the song.

I successfully made the minor transition into the chorus and continued into the second verse and second chorus, then moved into the bridge and the final chorus.

But I'm a creep, I'm a weirdo, what the hell am I doing here? I don't belong here. I don't belong here.

The final note concluded and the guitar feedback and bass faded until it was silent. I meticulously removed my fingers off the strings and raised my hands above my head as I stared at the spackled ceiling.

I counted three mistakes. Three total mistakes in a four-minute song—and I considered those minor blunders that probably would have gone unnoticed by an audience. I felt dumbfounded that I could go from having no musical capability to being able to play a complete song in the span of less than ninety days. After a few moments of inner celebration I finally looked up at Jake and prepared myself for his criticism.

"What did you think?"

"I think you played the song."

"I agree. What grade would you give it?"

"I'd give you a C."

"Only a C?"

"Yeah, you fucked up in a couple places that we'll work on, but overall I think it sounded good. I'm really fucking proud of you."

"Thanks. I couldn't have done it without you."

"Shut up and let's keep fucking playing."

"Creep" was on repeat until sunrise.

After that all-night session I became obsessed with practice. I practiced at every possible opportunity I had. I practiced before work, after work, before bed, while I watched TV sitting on my bed, and sometimes even while on the toilet. I continued practicing the fundamentals but was also learning songs like "Vasoline" by Stone Temple Pilots, "Thunder Kiss '65" by White Zombie, "Cherub Rock" by Smashing Pumpkins, and "Far Behind" by Candlebox.

I don't know when it happened, but one day everything came together and things just clicked. I could play. I could actually play. It was starting to become second nature. I knew I was in the early stages of a very long journey to becoming a musician, but I had taken the first steps, and each day I was getting closer and closer.

On a wintry January night after a few hours of practice and multiple beers I opened a black Mead notebook and began drafting a musical checklist. I finished the checklist with nine items I was going to strive for, ranging from achievable to nearly impossible.

I crossed off the first item and tore the page out of the notebook. I folded up the paper and stuffed it into my wallet.

Music Checklist

Learn to play
Join a band
Play a show
Record an album
Go on tour
Play a show with a national band
Play a sold-out show
Get signed to a record label
Play Red Rocks

License to III

(Or Chapter 3)

April 1999 – October 1999

Band Number One
Genre: Alternative rock, rap rock and nu-metal
Influences: 311, Incubus, Limp Bizkit, and the Beastie Boys
Members: Seth–guitars, vocals; Cody–guitars, vocals, turntables;
Jake–drums

"I think it's time to start looking for a band," said Jake.

"Are you fucking kidding me? I'm not ready to play with anyone else yet."

"You're better than you think. And you're only going to get better when you play with other musicians, especially ones who are better than you."

"Well, it won't be tough finding musicians better than me."

"You're ready, I promise."

I knew Jake was disregarding my objection. He wanted to start a band, and he wanted me to be the bass player—that was his primary motive for teaching me. I was content having our one-on-one practice sessions for the foreseeable future, and the thought of playing in front of anyone other than Jake was terrifying. I wasn't prepared to play with other talented musicians, I wasn't even prepared to play with *average* musicians.

Three days later Jake handed me a folded-up piece of paper. "Take a look at this," he said.

I looked at him, then the paper, then I slowly unfolded it.

2 Guitar Players Looking for Drummer & Bass Player
Influences include Rock, Alternative and Hip Hop
Must have Equipment and Stage Experience

"What do you think about this?"

"No," I said, fixated on the paper. "Please just give me another few months."

"I'll give you four days."

"What are you talking about?" I said as I slowly moved my eyes from the paper and back to Jake.

"I already called them. We're going to jam on Friday."

"Are you fucking serious!?"

"Yeah."

"I fucking hate you so much right now."

"You'll thank me later."

The two guitar players from the flyer were Seth and Cody, and both of them had been playing guitar since their early teens. They had been in numerous bands by the time they reached their early twenties, and combined they had over fifteen years of guitar-playing experience. I barely had five months.

Seth, a twentysomething Californian, was a recent Colorado transplant. He talked fast, listened selectively, and reminisced about the ocean. Cody was a native Coloradan and was in the same high school graduating class as Jake and I. I'd had a few classes with him, and we were friendly, but I didn't consider us friends. We ran with different crowds and our paths rarely crossed.

Cody already knew Jake was a talented drummer so Jake didn't have to audition, but my musical abilities were in question and would require a tryout. It would be my moment to shine or go down in flames.

"I know you're probably really nervous right now, but trust me, you can play," Jake said on the drive to the audition." You've done it in front of me hundreds of times and you'll do great. Just have confidence in yourself and play like it's me and you in your bedroom."

I looked at him and wanted to respond, but I couldn't think of anything to say so I nodded silently. I was terrified. I felt nauseous and considered jamming a finger down my throat to induce vomiting in hopes it would ease my nerves.

I had flashbacks of my third-grade spelling bee and the stage fright I had when my name was called. I looked out onto the entire student body, teachers, faculty, parents, and family members—and became paralyzed with stage fright. I looked at the moderator as he announced the word, then I looked out onto the vast audience. After a long pause, I opened my mouth and uttered the letters S-I-R-K-U-S.

"I am sorry Scott, that is incorrect. The correct spelling is C-I-R-C-U-S, circus." The moderator's voice echoed through the PA speakers in the gymnasium. I turned around and sheepishly walked off the stage to random giggles from the audience. That word was the embodiment of my personal failure. I had no idea how the audition was going to proceed, but I envisioned myself not being able to play a single note and having to exit in the same embarrassing fashion as I did during the spelling bee.

The audition was in the living room of Cody's second-story, one-bedroom apartment. After an introduction to Seth and brief conversation over a beer, everyone proceeded to the living room.

The size of the apartment and proximity to neighbors didn't allow for us to set up a guitar amp, PA, and drums, so I played my Ibanez through a six-inch Peavey practice amp while Cody and Seth played on acoustic guitars. I sat next to Jake on a couch across from Cody and Seth, who began tuning their guitars in preparation to play. I watched as they casually strummed their guitars, making it look effortless, and I knew I was a greenhorn about to play with seasoned veterans.

I removed my bass from the gig bag and noticed my right hand trembling. I was inept, unconfident, and inexperienced—a dangerous combination.

"I gotta take a piss real quick," I said as I stood up from the couch.

I was stalling, searching for something, anything that would give me the confidence to play beyond my capability. I had the feeling whatever it was wouldn't be found in a cheap apartment bathroom mirror, but I went to the bathroom anyway. I stood in front of the toilet and attempted to pee, but a steady stream didn't flow. It was a drizzle, and the majority landed on my boxers and Levi's. I spent two minutes dabbing and drying the spots with toilet paper.

I returned to the living room and quickly sat down and grabbed my bass. I took a deep breath, cracked my knuckles and began warming up with the bass scales Jake taught me. After a few minutes I stopped and looked up to Seth and Cody.

"Do you want to try an original or do a cover?" Seth asked.

"I'm good with either," I said.

"Let's try an original. We have a new one that's pretty simple and should be easy to learn."

"Perfect."

"Do you want us to break down each section or should we just play it and you jump in whenever?"

"Play it and I'll come in once I got it," I responded.

"Sounds good."

"1, 2, 3," Seth said then, both of them started to play.

The next hour and a half was a blur. I vaguely remember attempting to learn three originals and one cover song. I failed miserably at everything. Seth and Cody continued switching songs, searching for one that I could somewhat play. It was to no avail. I felt like I was back in my bedroom with Jake on that first night of practice.

"We'll be in touch," Cody said as we walked out of the apartment. I had a feeling he wouldn't.

Jake and I walked through the parking lot to my car in silence. His demeanor confirmed how disastrous the audition actually went.

"Circus—fucking circus," I whispered to myself.

"What?"

"Nothing. How bad was it?"

Jake paused, searching for something encouraging, "I thought you started playing good on that last song."

"That bad huh?"

"It could have been worse."

"How so?"

"Let me get back to you on that one."

I arrived home a little after midnight and sat in silence on the edge of my bed. Failing so miserably was a gut punch, and I considered breaking the Ibanez into pieces and using it for firewood. I became consumed with self-doubt, and self-doubt can be debilitating and a dream killer. Self-doubt is what almost made me destroy this book sometime during the third draft.

"Let's give it one more try," I said as I reached for my bass guitar and notebook.

I decided at that moment I wasn't going to be mediocre, and I wasn't going to embarrass myself again. I made a promise to myself that if I ever got another audition for another band I would be prepared and ready to play.

The next day Seth called Jake and they discussed the audition.

"Scott sucks, but we want you to play drums for us," Seth said to Jake.

"I promise he can play. I've seen him, he's good. He just had an off night."

"Off night? It looked like that was the first time he's ever played. I don't think it could have sounded worse."

"Give him one more shot."

"I really don't see the point."

"It's either both of us or neither of us. You guys pick."

After a short pause, Seth finally responded. "Okay, we'll give him one more audition."

The second audition was two weeks later, and I prepared for it like a 4.0 high school student prepares for the SAT. I had notes from the first audition and spent hours practicing each verse, chorus, bridge, and transition of the three original songs over, and over, and over.

"That was a lot better," Seth said after we completed the first song uninterrupted.

"Thanks. I've been practicing."

Three hours after the start of the second audition, I was invited to join the band. The conversation shifted to possible band names and practice locations.

I was standing in a strip-mall parking lot surrounded by a Chinese restaurant, laundromat, liquor store, veterinary clinic, and about ten other small businesses, including a music venue with a dimly lit maroon-and-yellow rectangular sign that read, "ECK'S SALOON."

Eck's was located in Lakewood, a suburb southwest of Denver, and though it labeled itself a hard rock venue, it was a quintessential dive bar. It was the type of place you could routinely hear customers doing lines of cocaine in the bathroom stalls and where fights broke out almost as frequently as the daily happy hour. I lived less than ten minutes from Eck's and usually kept my distance, but I had to change my policy because they were the first venue to offer us a show.

"You guys will get a forty-minute set, and each member gets two free draft beers," the venue manager told us.

That was a king's ransom for us, especially considering most venues wouldn't even return our calls. At that point I would have paid to play, so we graciously accepted the offer to play in exchange for twenty-four dollars' worth of beer.

The show was on Tuesday, October 14, about four months after our first official practice, and thirteen days after my twenty-third birthday. I was about to perform in front of an audience for the first time, a feat Jake, Seth, and Cody all accomplished as a teenager. The closest I ever came to a public performance was a skit I acted out in an American History class during my senior year of high school.

I sat alone at a table in front of the stage and opened a notebook that included tablature for all nine songs on the set list. I nervously flipped through the frayed pages, executing a last-minute cram session of the simple, no-frills bass lines designed to minimize the possibility of mistakes.

Twenty-minutes later, I was summoned onto the stage to set up my equipment. My setup was simple because my equipment consisted of only three key pieces: a 4x10 Peavey cabinet, a Peavey amplifier, and my Ibanez bass guitar. The setup process was straightforward: plug the amp into a power supply, then plug the guitar into the amplifier, then plug the amplifier into the cabinet and turn the power on.

Jake had the most complex setup because his five-piece black Pearl drum kit included a snare drum, two rack toms, a floor tom, a bass drum, a hi-hat stand, a snare drum stand, two boom cymbal stands, a crash cymbal stand, a hi-hat, a fourteen-inch and eighteen-inch crash cymbal, a ride cymbal, bass drum pedal, a drum stool, three pairs of drumsticks, and numerous other miscellaneous pieces of equipment and hardware.

"Want to give me a hand?" Jake asked, engulfed in a mountain of drums.

"Sure."

I was clueless. I stared at the drums then finally picked up the cymbal bag. I removed a cymbal and started to place it on a cymbal stand.

"That's wrong. The smaller crash goes on the left and the bigger one goes on the right," he said, barely glancing up.

"Sorry," I responded. I began loosening the wing nut on the cymbal stand.

"How are you feeling?"

"This is pretty cool."

"Nervous, scared? Need to go rub one out in the bathroom?"

"Nah, I think I'm good. I honestly don't really feel anything."

"I think that's a good sign."

"I hope so."

"Don't sweat it. You're going to do awesome."

The sound guy walked onto the stage and introduced himself, I vaguely remember his name as Bob. He was overweight, haggard, and wore a faded Kiss T-shirt that was covered in stains and looked like it hadn't been washed in years. He had the stench of cheap bourbon and Marlboro Reds.

"You guys are going to sound amazing," Bob said. "I've been doing this for twenty years and toured with Blue Oyster Cult in the seventies. I'm one of the best sound guys in town."

I was tempted to ask why he was working at a dive bar instead of a large venue if he was one of the best, but I didn't want to cause any discord with the first sound guy of my career. "Great, I'm sure it's going to sound awesome," I said as he walked away, uninterested in hearing my answer.

I watched as Bob miked the entire drum kit, a task that took nearly twenty-minutes. When he was done there were seven microphones attached to the kit along with two overhead microphones.

I was thankful I didn't decide to become a drummer. For starters, I didn't have the talent to be one, and second, drumming is the hardest position in any rock band. Being a competent drummer requires skill, practice, technique, finesse, rhythm, timing, musical knowledge, and limb independence—meaning that each of the drummer's limbs can play different rhythms simultaneously without focusing on each one individually. It's not something that can be learned in mere months.

Next Bob miked the guitars, bass, turntables, and set up two vocal microphones on either side of the stage. He then stepped off stage and schlepped to the soundboard beyond the dance floor.

"Can I get the kick?" Bob asked through the stage monitor speakers as he jammed a cigarette into an ashtray next to the soundboard.

Jake started stepping on the bass drum pedal and continued until Bob was satisfied with the sound. They repeated this for the snare and each tom, then Jake played the entire drum kit. The process took about ten minutes.

"Can I get stage left"? Bob asked next.

I had heard that term before, but I was unsure if it meant left from the viewpoint of someone standing onstage or from the viewpoint of someone standing in front of the stage. I pointed to myself with confusion.

"Yes, bass player, you are stage left. Please play something so I can get your levels."

"Sorry," I said. I dropped my head and quickly started playing.

Thirty seconds passed. "Bass sounds good, can I get stage right guitar?" I pressed mute on my amp and watched as the rest of the band completed their soundcheck.

"You guys go on in twenty-minutes," he announced.

I was twenty-minutes from commencing my musical career and probably should have done something celebratory, but I just went to the bathroom, cracked my fingers, and waited at the side of the stage.

Moments before our set the band did a pre-show huddle then everyone rushed onto the stage. I strapped my bass on, un-muted the volume, and turned to face the audience.

There were about fifty people scattered throughout the dance floor, bar, and pool area. About half of them were family and friends who were there to see us, and the other half didn't give a fuck that a band was about to play and preferred to hear music from the jukebox.

The house PA music faded, and the room became so quiet you could hear pool balls colliding. Seth walked up to his microphone and was about to speak when someone in the audience broke the silence for him.

"Play Freebird!" they shouted. This was followed by drunken laughter.

I hadn't even played the first song of my first show and already I was getting heckled with one of the most cliché requests in rock 'n' roll. I guess it was a badge of honor.

Jake clicked his drumsticks together, signaling the start of our first song. I stared down at my bass and started to play. Adrenaline was rushing through my body, and I could feel myself playing too fast. I attempted to relax and play at the correct tempo, but I was unsure if I succeeded.

I didn't look up from my bass once, but at the conclusion of the first song I glanced back at Jake. He nodded and gave me a thumbs-up. Then I heard applause and turned towards the crowd. I was awestruck standing on that small stage. It was one of those moments you wish could last forever, but it only lasted mere seconds because our second song started before the applause ended.

An hour later, I was standing at the bar surrounded by friends drinking Bud Lights. I was on a euphoric high. I had dreamed about this day for years and had spent countless hours wondering what it would feel like to perform with a band in front of an audience. It exceeded all expectations.

I was about to signal the bartender for a round of whiskey shots when my friend John tapped me on the shoulder.

"Hey, there's some guy talking shit about you to Jake and your guitar player," he said.

"Are you fucking serious?"

I rotated the stool 90-degrees and spotted Jake and Seth at a table with two guys I had never seen before. I jumped off the stool and ran to the table.

"I'm telling you—if you kick out that other guitar player and bass player you guys have a real fucking shot at going somewhere. With those two, you have no fucking chance," the guy slurred as I approached from behind.

"What the fuck did you say?" I said as I tapped him on the shoulder.

The guy paused for a moment, then turned and stood up. I was not a small guy—about six feet tall, weighing around 210 pounds—but this guy towered over me. He was at least four or five inches taller and probably had twenty pounds on me. He also had a muscular build with biceps as large as my neck. I was not looking forward to the possibility of a fight with this guy and questioned my decision to intervene in the conversation.

"I want to know what the fuck you're saying," I said in my tough-guy voice. I hoped he would be intimidated with my tough-guy act. It didn't work.

"It doesn't concern you," he said as he jammed his index finger into my chest.

"Fuck you!" I said as I shoved his finger off my chest. "If you're talking to my band, it does concern me."

"Well if you must know, I was just telling these guys you and that other guitar player fucking suck."

He was partially correct. His opinion of me was somewhat accurate, but his opinion of Cody was entirely wrong. I was about to respond when the tone of the conversation quickly escalated—and it escalated with a punch to the temple from John, who lunged at the guy from two tables away. John was drunk and the punch barely connected, but the guy still fell back into a table and two chairs, knocking over the table, chairs, and glasses before he hit the ground.

The guy instantaneously sprung to his feet and charged at me. I turned to my left and grabbed the closest object within reach, which turned out to be a barstool. I picked it up by the legs and swung for the fences with my eyes closed.

I felt it connect with someone and was thrilled, but that excitement quickly dissipated after I opened my eyes and realized the person I hit was wearing a shirt with "Security" written boldly across the front. The security guard was the size of an NFL offensive lineman and the barstool barely rattled him. He looked at me and concluded I was not a threat and turned his attention to the drunk guy. He swiftly subdued the drunk guy, and the melee ended as fast as it started. The drunk guy, his friend, and John were kicked out of Eck's. I assumed at the very least I would be kicked out for accidentally assaulting an employee, but the security guard gently placed his hand on my shoulder.

"Sorry about that. That guy is always here starting shit. I should know better by now."

"It's okay. Sorry about hitting you with a chair."

"Don't worry about that. Let me get you a beer," he said.

That was the moment I became aware of the benefits that come from being the talent.

Shout at the Devil

(Or Chapter 4)

November 1999 – January 2001

After our first show at Eck's, we began playing the Monday and Tuesday night bar circuit. Each show was usually only attended by the staff, bar regulars, members of the other bands we played with and their friends, and the friends and family we begged to attend.

"If you come, I'll buy you a drink," I'd say to anyone who showed the slightest interest in attending.

I was optimistic that once the person arrived they would enjoy the music enough to forget the barter. I purchased a lot of drinks in the beginning of our run.

Almost every band starts on a weeknight circuit until they can prove they're worthy of a weekend slot. The music actually isn't a major factor, but how many people a band can get through the door is. The venue's rationale is monetary: the more people in attendance at a show means there will be more alcohol consumed, which in turn produces higher bar sales and generates more revenue for the venue. Some venues would rather book an atrocious band that can get a hundred people through the door than a talented band that's struggling to get twenty.

Over time, the talented bands usually rise to the top and start gathering a following and begin getting offers to play better and higher-profile shows. The lousy bands usually become stagnant because you can only ask family, friends, and coworkers so many times before they start making excuses for why they can't come.

In the early days, we yearned to perform on stage and play anywhere that agreed to have us. This included dive bars, white trash bars, house parties, fraternity parties, dilapidated theaters, battle of the bands, bars without a stage or sound system, raves, a DIY music festival in a dirt field, and even a seedy strip club that instructed us to play stuff that the dancers could "shake their ass to." The show results varied.

After eight months of constant practicing and performing, our songs got better, the music got tighter, and the audiences started to grow. The crowds went from twenty or thirty people to fifty or a hundred, and venues started asking us to play on the weekends. The hours of hard work were paying off and we rose from being a subpar band to an average band to a quality band.

We started making some money. Not a lot, but enough to start a band fund: fifty dollars here, seventy-five dollars there. Occasionally, we would walk away with a few hundred. This fund allowed us to move out of a garage with time and noise restrictions to a dedicated practice space that allowed us to play music twenty-four hours a day, seven days a week.

The practice spot was located in an alley between Broadway Boulevard and Lincoln Street, in the basement of a vacant office building three blocks south of the Colorado State Capitol building. We named it "the Boiler Room," because it contained a rickety 1950s–era industrial boiler in the back of the room. It was enormous, five feet by ten feet, and from the look of it, probably emitted toxic fumes. I also surmised the walls contained lead paint and the insulation was made with asbestos. Spending a myriad of hours in that room was probably not ideal for our overall health.

The Boiler Room was only accessible from the alley through a wooden door that led to an old, creaking wooden staircase with steps that were different lengths, heights, and angles. It was a challenge to navigate while blindly carrying music equipment to the bottom floor, especially after a few drinks.

The rent was $250 a month, which was paid from the band fund. Occasionally there wasn't enough money in the fund, so the remaining balance was split evenly between each member: sometimes twenty dollars, sometimes fifty, and a few times, the entire balance.

The Boiler Room not only gave us a place to practice, but it also served as a band meeting room, a band marketing room, a merchandise room, a storage room, and a place to throw parties. It became my home away from home.

The room measured around twenty feet wide by forty feet long and was larger than some of the venues we played. It could easily accommodate thirty people, and on most weekends it did. Some nights we would arrive with a couple cases of beer and throw a party because we could be as loud and as rowdy as we wanted to be. We were forming new friendships and relationships within the cold, dim toxic cement walls.

Sometime in January of 2000, a girl named Amy maneuvered down the staircase and sat on the couch directly across from me. I was enthralled, and my eyes fixated on her smile for the rest of the night.

Amy was friends with a girl Cody was dating, and their group of friends started coming to the Boiler Room on a regular basis. On every occasion I flirted with Amy, but initially she didn't show the slightest bit of interest. I didn't blame her. I was lowest on the band dating hierarchy. The order started with the vocalist, then the guitar player, then the drummer, and finally, the bass player. This hierarchy is obviously subject to different factors, but on a level playing field, bass players usually have the least amount of dating potential. I've never overheard a woman brag to her friends that she was dating a bass player. Unfortunately for me, I *was* the bass player, and the least talented and attractive member of the band to boot.

But I was persistent, and she finally conceded and gave me her phone number after we woke up together on Cody's couch following a long night of drinking. I utilized the three-day rule, then called the number, half expecting to hear a disconnected message. It rang, and rang, and rang a few more times. The line finally picked up, then there was a quick pause and her voicemail message started playing. I hesitated, unsure what to say. I proceeded to leave a mundane, unwitty, and awkward message.

I waited one day, then two days, then five days, finally giving up hope after a week had gone by.

Eleven days after the initial call, my phone rang and her name appeared on the caller ID. I was reluctant to answer. Eleven days to return a call was a red-flag that she wasn't interested. I was unsure why she was calling, but I answered, and we made small talk until she broke the tedious conversation.

"Do you wanna hang out tonight?"

"Sure," I responded without hesitation.

We had our first kiss that night and began dating a week later.

The first time I entered a recording studio was over a weekend in December of 1999, when I visited Time Capsule Studios. Time Capsule was not a top-tier studio frequented by high-profile rockstars. It was a single-story house with a detached garage in a middle-class neighborhood in Lakewood, Colorado. The control room was in the basement of the house and the live recording room was across the driveway in a converted detached garage. It wasn't glamorous, but at twenty dollars an hour it was all we could afford.

We had approximately $500 in the band fund, and that allotted us twenty-five hours of recording, mixing, and mastering time. Our plan was to record music for six songs on Saturday, and come back on Sunday to record the vocals, then mix and master with the remaining time. I was a complete recording novice, but that schedule felt ambitious and optimistic.

We arrived that Saturday morning to the recording engineer sitting in an office chair in front of a large mixing board with hundreds of different-colored sliders, rotary knobs, buttons, faders and different-sized inputs. There were gain controls, volume faders, equalizer controls, pre- and post-auxiliary controls, pain controls, mute buttons, and an assortment of other controls whose purpose I had no idea of. It looked as complicated as a Boeing 747 cockpit.

Along with the mixing board, there was an assortment of microphones, countless feet of colored cables of different lengths, microphone stands, music stands, numerous pairs of headphones, and a surplus of extra equipment that included guitars, basses, amplifiers, and cabinets.

Jake set up his drums, and within an hour he was recording the first song. Recording drums is usually the most time-consuming instrument due to the tedious set up process, and the high degree of difficulty that results in a greater probability of error. Jake was a professional though, and he finished the six songs in a breakneck pace. I was on-deck, and unlike Jake, I wasn't confident in my abilities.

As I stood alone in the garage with my bass over my shoulder and headphones over my ears I worried that the allotted two hours wasn't enough time for me to record all the bass parts for six songs. I still felt like an inadequate bass player and somehow I was deceiving the rest of the band. I pictured myself attempting to record the first song, only to fail take after take and finally be exposed as the fraud that I was.

"Are you ready?" the engineer's voice came into the headphones.

"Yeah—I think so."

I recorded all six songs in one hour and thirty-five minutes. As soon as I removed the headphones my insecurities as a bass player started to dissipate.

By the end of that Sunday we spent almost twenty-three hours recording, mixing, and mastering the six songs. We handed the engineer a check for $480 and he handed us a cassette tape with the word "demo" written on a white label.

Holding the tape was one of the proudest moments of my life, but my pride quickly diminished after listening to the cassette a few times. There were obvious issues ranging from problems with tempo and pitch to incorrect notes to the mixing of the songs. We rushed the recording process, and the result was an amateurish-sounding EP.

We sold zero copies of this record, because we released zero copies. It sounded like shit, and I didn't expect anyone to pay for it. We initially gave it away to whoever wanted it, but the tape was eventually packed away into a box with my other music memorabilia. Nirvana recorded their first album, *Bleach,* in thirty-hours at a cost of $606. We were no Nirvana.

A few weeks after the recording session we played a show to a crowd of about fifty people. After our set a friend introduced us to a guy named Jim.

"You guys were really good. I see a lot of potential," he said.

Jim went on to tell us that he had built a recording studio in his basement and was looking for a band to record. He did this as a hobby and distraction from his day job as an aviation accident investigator. His job required him to go to plane crash scenes and determine what caused the crash, recording was a way for Jim to forget the death and destruction he saw.

I was skeptical about recording at another home studio with a hobbyist at the controls, but we agreed to visit the studio and listen to his previous recordings. Sixty seconds into the first song I turned to Jake and nodded.

After listening to six or seven songs, Jim turned to all of us and proposed that we record the full-length CD in his studio for free. I thought I misheard him, until he repeated it.

"My day job pays the bills so I don't need the money. I just want to record a really good band and put out a really good album," he said.

It was a no-brainer. We agreed with a handshake deal to record, mix, and master fifteen songs during the months of April and May of 2000—for the whopping cost of nothing.

We spent the next four months refining our songs, and we walked into that studio brimming with confidence. We were stress-free, partially because of our rigorous practice schedule and partially because the recording session wasn't going to cost a cent.

I had multiple days to record, which allowed me time to perfect my bass parts with the record button pressed. I was able to listen back to my recordings, and then scrutinize every intro, every verse, every chorus, and any other section of our songs until I was 100 percent satisfied with the recording. The recording would be finished when it sounded perfect, not when we ran out of time or money.

The schedule was to record drums, then bass, then rhythm guitar, then lead guitar, then vocals for Seth, then vocals for Cody. Recording the turntables and some miscellaneous percussion would be the final touches.

Jake finished recording the drum parts in two weeks and I began tracking bass on the third Monday of April. I sat on a stool across from Jim and we started the extensive process of writing, recording, deleting, re-recording, and repeating, and repeating—and repeating.

If I played the wrong note I heard, "Play that one again." If I got off tempo I heard, "Try that slower next time." If things just didn't sound right, "How about we try that again? I think you can do it better." Recording will magnify your deficiencies and give you no place to hide. Take after take after take, hours upon hours of hearing the same song and same parts hundreds of times until the song was perfect. It was monotonous and exhausting but immensely rewarding when a song was finished and crossed off the dry-erase board.

Eight days and five separate sessions later, Jim said the bittersweet phrase, "You're done."

The next four weeks were spent recording the guitars, vocals, and additional percussion and after a total of seven weeks of intensive recording sessions, we were finished. The band wouldn't play another note as the album moved to the mixing and mastering phase.

Mixing is the process of adjusting and combining the individual audio tracks into a single stereo audio file. A simple, non-musician explanation is that vocals, guitars, drums, and other instruments are recorded separately on individual tracks, and the mixing process combines those tracks into a single song.

Mastering is the process of optimizing a song by using equalization, compression, limiting and other processes. A simple, non-musician explanation is that mastering makes the music louder, cleaner and improves the overall sound quality. Mixing and mastering is required if you want to have a professional-sounding song or album.

On the first Friday of June, Jim gave me the mastered copy of our finished full-length CD, and I could not have been more excited. I listened to the album on repeat for the entire weekend, probably twenty or thirty times. Over, and over, and over again, appreciating it more with every listen.

We booked our CD release for Saturday, July 15, at the Ogden Theatre on Colfax Avenue, seven blocks east of the capitol. It was built in 1917 and had once hosted a performance by Harry Houdini. The Ogden had a capacity of about 1,100 and was the largest room we ever booked—almost twice the size.

It was intimidating. If a hundred people attended one of our shows, it was considered a success. If a hundred people attended the CD release, the Ogden would be less than 10 percent full, and the show would be considered a failure and an embarrassment. To this day, my biggest fear as a musician is playing to an empty venue.

We carefully selected three opening bands based primarily on their fan base and local draw. Then we carefully selected the date, because there is nothing worse than booking and promoting a show only to realize it's the same night a larger, more popular band is playing or a blizzard is headed into town.

It was scheduled for mid-July, so the chance of snow was close to zero, and the weekend concert schedule was unusually light. A local indie rock show was happening two miles east at the Bluebird Theater, but that was a different genre, so that show would have little effect on our audience.

We printed hundreds of flyers and thousands of handbills. The handbills were given to every person that would take them and the flyers were taped to every imaginable location in the Denver metro area: record stores, music stores, head shops, bookstores, coffee shops, telephone poles, streetlight poles, bulletin boards at all the local colleges, and what felt like every independent music store within a twenty-five mile radius of the

Ogden. Concert promotion was becoming a second job and we spent a small fortune on gas and rolls of tape.

Our plan was to plaster the city with our flyers. If someone who enjoyed music or coffee, or someone purchasing a pipe didn't show up, it wouldn't be because they didn't know about the CD release party—it would be because they didn't care we were playing. Either way, they would know.

Around 5:00 p.m. on CD release Saturday the opening band arrived at the Ogden and began loading onto the stage. I watched them perform soundcheck then walked to the front lobby and peeked out the front entrance, where a small line of eight people had formed. It was the first show I ever played that had a line.

I then walked to the merchandise counter and stared at the boxes and boxes of CDs and the assortment of T-Shirts hanging behind the counter. I grabbed a shirt and brought it to my face, inhaling the smell of the freshly printed ink. For the first time in our band's short career, I felt we had the appearance of a semi-professional act. I was finally starting to get excited, but the excitement would last less than ten minutes.

Thirty-minutes prior to doors opening, and an hour before the opening band was scheduled to start, the venue went dark. The only light in the building illuminated from the fire exits signs. It took me a minute for my eyes to adjust to the darkness, and while that was happening I noticed the room was strangely quiet. No amps, no music, no air conditioner, and no hum of the building. The only sounds that could be heard were confused conversations and vehicles driving past the theater on Colfax Avenue.

I noticed a beam of light shining onto the lobby floor and saw a group of Ogden employees congregating. I discreetly walked up to them and leaned in to eavesdrop.

"The power for the whole fucking building is out. It looks like it's out for the entire block," an employee said.

"That's fucking crazy! Has this ever happened before?"

"I don't think so."

"What are we supposed to do?"

"I guess call Xcel and wait."

Xcel is the local power company, and what we didn't know was that they had initiated a brownout due to large electrical power draws stemming from the day's 99-degree temperature and excessive use of air conditioning units. The brownout is an effort to reduce load and prevent a total power outage.

It was supposed to be our triumphant CD release party, but since there wasn't enough electricity to power all of the air conditioners and household fans in Denver, our night was about to turn into a colossal fucking disaster.

"Power is history," I said to Cody, Seth, and Jake.

"Is it going to come back on?" Cody asked.

"From what I gathered nobody has any fucking clue."

"What the fuck are we going to do?" Seth asked.

I slowly raised my hands and shrugged, half in frustration and half in amusement.

"I could set up my drums and play to kill some time," Jake said.

"That's not a bad idea," said Cody.

"I have a few things that might be perfect for something like this."

"I say do it," I replied.

"Okay!"

Jake ran to the drummer of the opening band and explained his idea, and they formulated a performance within a few minutes. They both jumped onto the stage and started setting up their drums, the only light coming from the back door. By the time they were finished setting up, there were about fifty people scattered throughout the venue.

Jake walked to the front of the stage and yelled, "We're going to play you some improvised drums until the power comes back on! Hope you guys enjoy it."

He then walked behind his kit, clicked his drumsticks together and shouted, "One, two, three!"

It started off rough, but once they got into a groove it sounded tight, almost like they had been practicing the routine for weeks.

"This actually sounds really good," Seth said.

"Hopefully they can keep it up for a while," I responded.

About five minutes into the performance the venue manager tapped me on the shoulder and asked us to come to the lobby.

"I just got the word the power is going to be out for at least a few hours. We're going to have to cancel the show. Sorry guys."

"Fuck," the three of us said almost in unison.

I slouched against the wooden merchandise counter as sweat dripped down my forehead and into my eyes. I helplessly watched as staff escorted people out of the Ogden, onto the sidewalk and into the sunlight. An employee taped a piece of paper on the entrance door:

Tonight's Show is Canceled Due to Power Outage

We loaded our equipment out of the Ogden and gathered in the parking lot behind the venue. I sat on the tailgate of my truck drinking a Bud Light and kicking the air in frustration.

"All that time and money promoting down the fucking drain," I said.

"Stupid fucking Xcel!" Jake yelled as he threw a beer can against the towering cement wall of the Ogden.

"What are we going to do now?"

"I don't know about you, but I'm going to get really drunk," Jake said as he opened a beer and walked away.

I laid into the bed of the truck, closed my eyes, and contemplated getting drunk and passing out in the parking lot.

"Scott! Is that you?" a somewhat-familiar voice shouted across the parking lot.

I crouched up and saw my friend Rachel and a little kid walking towards me.

"What the heck is going on? There's a sign on the front door that says the show is canceled because of a power failure?" Rachel said.

"That's correct."

"Seriously?"

I nodded methodically.

"Well that really sucks! This was going to be Mike's first concert ever," she said as she pointed to the kid, who looked to be about ten.

"Sorry little guy, but there isn't going to be a show tonight."

He smiled.

"I guess we'll just go grab some ice cream then. Do you want to join?" Rachel asked.

"No, I think I'm going to drown my sorrows here, but thanks for the invite and thanks for coming."

I gave her a hug and extended my hand to offer Mike a high five.

"Could . . . could I still buy a CD?" Mike nervously asked.

"Wait right here!"

I grabbed a CD from the merchandise box and handed it to him.

"Here you go! It's yours for coming down here," I said.

"Thanks so much! Will you guys sign it?" Mike inquired, offering it back to me.

"Of course."

The CD release show was rescheduled for Saturday, August 5. The overall vibe was less enthusiastic and less climactic. We had put so much time, money, and effort into promoting the original date, it was tough to replicate. We also had to scramble to find adequate opening band replacements because two of the bands from the original release party had to cancel due to scheduling conflicts.

On the night of the show the temperature was in the low nineties, there were no brownouts and the show went off without a hitch. We played to a crowd of about five hundred people, a little under 50 percent of the Ogden's capacity. Our merchandise sales included almost fifty CDs and a handful of shirts for a total of $550—a decent haul for a local band playing a local show.

The climax of the band was a 2000 New Year's Eve show at the Hard Rock Café on the 16th Street Mall in downtown Denver. Cody's girlfriend, Nina, had begun representing us over the summer as our booking manager and got us a headlining slot at the Hard Rock. She negotiated a free meal for each member, free drinks during the meal and a guaranteed payment of $2,000 for the performance—four times what we had ever made from a show.

We were booked to play two one-hour sets. The early one started at 9:00 p.m., then a DJ was going to perform until 11:45 p.m., and we would start our second set a little after midnight. The admission was twenty-five dollars a person, and that included a complementary glass of champagne. I was concerned it was too expensive, but the Hard Rock promised a full house.

I arrived at the Hard Rock around 7:00 p.m. and went upstairs to join the band for dinner. I ordered a burger, fries, and a Bud Light. I considered ordering something more expensive, but I was worried that we might have misunderstood the contract and would end up in a Blues Brothers situation where we couldn't afford the bill and would have to write a bad check to cover the food and drinks while exiting out the back entrance. I was waiting for someone to ask if we were the "Good Ole Boys."

After dinner I ventured outside and was astounded to see a line wrapping around the building. I started counting, but lost track about a third of the way into the line, at about fifty people.

"Holy fuck, are all these people coming to the show?" I asked Jake.

"It looks that way!" he said as he punched me in the shoulder.

"I guess I probably should've ordered more drinks."

A few weeks before the New Year's show I purchased an early Christmas present for myself, an orange Ernie Ball Music Man Stingray bass, and this was the first show I played with it. It was the first real, professional instrument I owned, and the same model was used by bassists like Flea from Red Hot Chili Peppers and Dave Farrell of Linkin Park.

The Hard Rock was sold-out an hour before our set, and by the time we walked onto the stage the two-story building was packed wall-to-wall on both floors. We turned the volume up and played loud, fast, and tight, and the crowd danced, drank, and celebrated the start of 2001. As the guitars faded at the conclusion of the second set, the crowd cheered the loudest applause I had ever heard on stage. It felt like it went on for minutes.

I was packing up my gear when Nina approached and handed me an envelope.

"Here's your cut," she said.

"Cut?"

"Your money from the show."

This was a rare moment because the only thing I was accustomed to getting after a show was a bar tab. I waited until she was out of eyesight and sheepishly opened the envelope. It contained $200. I didn't ask where the other $1,800 went, and I didn't care. For the first time in my musical career there was money that didn't have to go back into the band fund. I could finally call myself a paid musician.

Amy and I departed the Hard Rock before last call and wandered the streets of downtown Denver watching drunks stumble out of bars and last-minute hookup attempts. After awhile, the crowd thinned, and we sat on a bench and exchanged shots of Smirnoff out of a plastic cup in 20-degree weather while waiting for a taxi.

"I love you," Amy said.

"Love you too."

Twelve days after the Hard Rock show Cody abruptly quit the band. It happened after a show at a dive bar in north Denver that I ended after six songs because there were only eight people in the audience.

"This is bullshit. Let's skip to the last song in the set," I whispered to the band in between songs.

They stared at me in confusion for a few moments until they realized I was serious.

"I guess this is going to be our last song. Thanks for coming out," Seth announced to the audience.

The moment that song ended I took off my bass, turned off the amp, and preceded directly to the bar.

I've read interviews with famous musicians who said they didn't care if they played in front of ten people or ten thousand people. They just wanted a stage to perform their music, and if they had the opportunity to play in front of just one person, well, that was an opportunity to gain one more fan. They said they played exactly the same in front of an audience in a small dive bar as they would to an audience in an arena or stadium. Maybe this was true for them, but it was the polar opposite for me. If the audience wasn't at least a hundred people, I just didn't have the same energy and enthusiasm, and I'm sure it was obvious to anyone watching me.

Playing horrible shows to an audience of practically no one is rockstar training. It's paying your dues, learning how to perfect a craft, and becoming comfortable with your band, your instrument, and an audience. It's a classroom, and I wanted to ditch the entire semester and go straight to graduation. I was becoming proficient at my instrument, but I still had a lot to learn about becoming a true musician.

"I just don't have the time the band deserves," Cody said.

I knew he was upset about my unprofessional behavior during the post-New Year's show and would rather quit than play another show with me. We attempted to talk him out of leaving, but his mind was made up. He packed up his equipment and left the practice spot. Within the year he moved to Florida to pursue a recording career and has since been nominated for several Emmys for sound design on network television shows.

Seth, Jake, and I initially attempted to continue the band. We began an audition process, and after numerous tryouts we selected a guitar player, but he only lasted four months. We selected another guitar player—but he quit after six months. The band chemistry with the replacements never felt like it did with Cody, and the band never sounded the same after he left.

Seth decided to move home to Los Angeles and attempted to persuade Jake and I to move with him to reboot the band on the West Coast, but neither of us were mentally, emotionally, or financially prepared to move halfway across the country. We both declined.

"Give me a call if you ever make it out to California," Seth said the night before he moved.

"I will," I replied.

And just like that, after three and a half years, hundreds of shows, countless hours of practice, one EP, and one full-length CD, the band was over.

40 Oz. to Freedom

(Or Chapter 5)

February 2002 – October 2002

Band Number Two
Genre: Reggae and ska
Influences: Sublime, Slightly Stoopid, Pepper, and Less Than Jake
Members: Cameron—guitars, vocals; Doug—drums

I was sitting on a park bench during a break between Geology and Music Appreciation at Red Rocks Community College when my phone began to vibrate. I pulled the phone out of my pocket. It was a guy named Cameron.

Cameron had formed a band sometime in the late 1990s, and it had quickly become one of Denver's top reggae/ska bands, opening for national acts like Slightly Stoopid and Pepper. I had been to many of their shows over the years and they seemed to have a different bass player every time. I was friendly with Cameron, but I didn't consider us friends. I thought about sending the call to voicemail, but I answered it after the fourth ring. We made small talk for a few minutes until he got to the purpose of his call.

"So I heard you guys broke up," he said.

"I'd call it an extended hiatus."

"Would you be interested in a new project?"

"Maybe."

"Well we just parted ways with our bass player and I was wondering if you might be interested in jamming?"

I stared at a grass embankment for a moment then responded, "I haven't really thought about playing with anyone else. Can I think about it and get back to you in a few hours? I have to get to class."

"Yeah, but get back to me as soon as you can. We have a show booked in a few weeks and I'd like to find a replacement so I don't have to cancel it."

I wanted to say yes to the audition, but there was one roadblock, and that was Jake. I felt that if I joined another band I would be betraying him. He was the one who taught me how to play, he mentored me—and if it wasn't for him I would have never had the opportunity to play in the first band. If he hadn't talked Seth and Cody into giving me a second audition, I probably would have been so discouraged that I would have sold my guitar and never played music again.

Jake and I were searching for a new singer and guitar player to start a new band, or an existing band that needed a rhythm section. The search resulted in zero viable candidates, and I had a feeling that it could take months, or even years.

As much as I wanted to play music again, I felt indebted to him. The last thing I wanted to do was leave him high and dry.

Three weeks and six practices later I was standing on the stage of Herman's Hideaway, a small venue in central Denver that caters to local bands, most notably the Fray and Big Head Todd and the Monsters before they reached mainstream success.

I obsessively played the first verse and first chorus of our first song while I waited to soundcheck. I had only practiced with Cameron and Doug for about ten hours total, learning the eleven songs like someone cramming for a final exam.

"Bass player, can you play something?" the sound guy asked through the monitor speakers.

I nodded and began playing the bass line of the first song again. I glanced down at the set list taped to a monitor and barely recognized a majority of the eleven songs written with a Sharpie on a *Playboy* centerfold. I had cheat sheets taped onto the monitor and the floor surrounding it. I didn't know the names of the songs, and my only reference to each song was a number correlating to its order of appearance in the set. My fear was Cameron would go off script and I would be lost and not recognize the song until he was halfway through the first verse.

The venue was surprisingly packed for a Thursday night, with about 150 people in attendance, and about half of them were on the dance floor directly in front of us. There were a lot of faces I didn't recognize and I began to feel somewhat anxious. This was a new band, with new songs, and endless possibilities for musical mistakes.

I searched the crowd looking for Amy and found her sitting at a table in the back of the venue with a few of her friends. I waved timidly and she raised her hands above her head and formed a heart shape. The endearing gesture temporarily helped ease my anxiety.

I started searching the crowd again, this time looking for Jake. I invited him multiple times and even wrote his name on the guest list, but I didn't see him, and my anxiety slowly returned. I had never played a show without him being five feet away, and I felt like I was missing my security blanket. If I got in trouble, I wouldn't have him to bail me out. I was standing on stage next to Cameron and Doug, but I essentially felt alone.

"I'm really excited for you," Jake said during a phone call two days before the show.

"You swear you're not mad?"

"I promise."

I didn't believe him, but I didn't blame him either. I didn't tell him that I was going on an audition. I had waited until I was a confirmed member to give him the news that our band was officially over. I was selfish, and a coward.

"Are you going to try to come?" I asked, almost pleading.

"I don't know yet. I have to work early on Friday."

"It would mean a lot if you were there."

"I'll try my hardest."

He didn't come, and I didn't talk to him again for months. Playing in a new band fractured my longest friendship.

As Cameron finished tuning his guitar he turned to Doug, then me and nodded, indicating he was ready to play. I gave a thumbs-up and walked to the front of the stage. The music coming through the PA slowly faded as Cameron started strumming the rhythm of reggae guitar chords.

During this period my relationship with Amy continued to grow. I experienced a lot of firsts with her: my first time having sushi, my first time going on a vacation with a girlfriend, and my first time not cheating.

Friends and family thought we would get married, but the notion never crossed my mind, and we never discussed it. I felt like we both knew this was young-adult love and that the relationship was finite. I wasn't sure what I wanted out of a relationship or out of life at that point.

That spring Amy got pregnant and after a lengthy discussion we came to the mutual decision to get an abortion. It wasn't an easy choice for either of us, but we were confident it was the correct one.

It took place at a health clinic in an unassuming medical building in Aurora, Colorado. We arrived, checked in, then sat in the waiting room. I aimlessly flipped through a stack of outdated magazines and Amy stared blankly at the floor. I reached for her hand, and she grabbed mine and squeezed it with such force that I eventually lost feeling in my fingers.

"Amy?" a nurse said.

"I love you," Amy said to me.

"I love you too."

We kissed, and she stood up and walked toward the nurse. Then she vanished behind a lobby door. I sat and stared at a clock, and waited, and waited, and waited.

She finally appeared in the doorway of the waiting room, drugged and comatose-seeming. I rushed to her and we hugged for a long time in the lobby. On the drive home she was speechless and stared blankly out the window. An occasional tear would slowly slide down her cheek and drip onto her shirt. I attempted to comfort her, but it was hopeless. I was completely distraught as well.

We were in our early twenties, and it was the first real adult decision either of us had ever made. It was a traumatic experience for us as individuals and for our relationship, and I knew it would either bring us together or tear us apart.

The Vans Warped Tour was an annual punk rock music festival founded in 1995 that crisscrossed the United States and Canada. It was the largest traveling music festival in North America, with an annual attendance of over 750,000 people. It covered around fifty dates from late June until late August, and each stop featured forty to sixty bands and five to eight different stages.

The tour had numerous sponsors including Vans, Samsung, Apple, Hard Rock Café, and Ernie Ball. In addition to basses, Ernie Ball manufactures guitars, strings, and other musical accessories. They also conducted a Battle of the Bands on each tour stop, which gave local bands a chance to submit a song and compete for a spot on the Ernie Ball-sponsored stage.

I wasn't sure how bands were selected, but I pictured a group of music nerds gathered in a dark room for days smoking cigarettes and listening to hundreds of horrible bands, whittling them down to the top four from each city good enough to play on the Ernie Ball stage.

We submitted a song that I wrote the music for within the first week of joining the band. It was a straightforward pop-punk bass line that was basically a rip-off of blink-182 and Green Day and featured the enormously popular I–V–VI–IV chord progression used in hundreds of pop and pop-punk songs, most notably "Let It Be" by the Beatles. If you're going to steal a song, make sure it's a good one.

I opened up my AOL account to check my email on a Tuesday in early June when a subject line caught my eye:

Congratulations! You have been selected . . .

I assumed it was another free giveaway for Viagra or a Nigerian Prince informing me that I had just inherited millions. I reluctantly opened the email, preparing to delete it instantaneously.

Congratulations! You have been selected to play the Denver Warped Tour.

I looked away and rubbed my eyes, then turned back to the screen, peering at it with one eye open.

Your song was selected by a panel as one of the top songs. Show details will be included in a forthcoming email.

I readjusted the chair and sat in silence for a few moments then reached across the desk for my Nokia 3110 phone. I wasn't sure who I should call first, but after scrolling through my contacts I selected Amy's name and pressed the call button.

"Hello?"

"We won! We fucking won!"

"What are you talking about? What did you win?"

"The battle of the bands! We're playing Warped Tour!"

"Are you serious?"

"Yes! Fucking yes!"

That was the first time I had been recognized for my musical accomplishments by professionals and provided further validation that I wasn't a hack. It was a tremendous honor to be selected, and it provided the possibility of playing in front of thousands of people. It felt good.

That night, Amy and I, along with our friends Ken and Abby went to a local sports bar called Old Chicago to celebrate. We shared a large pepperoni pizza, drank a few pitchers of Bud Light, and did a celebratory kamikaze shot.

Around 10:00 p.m. I decided to call it a night because I had to work at 6:00 a.m. the following morning.

"Would you mind running me home real quick?" I asked Amy.

"Do you just want to take my car?"

"Are you sure?"

"Yeah, I'll get a ride home with Abby, and you can come to my house in the morning and I'll drive you to work."

Amy lived five blocks from the golf course where we both worked. I was a prep cook and she was a bartender, waitress, and an occasional beverage-cart girl. I knew if she stayed at Old Chicago she would be too hungover to wake up at 5:50 a.m., let alone drive me, so I planned to leave my place early and drop her car at her house then walk the five blocks to the golf course.

I said goodbye to Ken and Abby and walked into the parking lot with Amy.

"Be careful with this beauty," Amy said as she dropped her keys into my palm.

"This fucking clunker? I'll try," I said as I kicked the bumper of the rundown 1988 Toyota Corolla.

"Be careful. Something might fall off."

We both laughed as I leaned her against the car. We made out for a few minutes, to the dismay of the couple parked in the adjacent spot.

"See you in the morning," I said.

"I love you." She blew a kiss then turned away.

I awoke to the buzzing of my alarm and swung at the snooze button until I finally hit it on the third try. The digital numbers displayed 5:01. I rolled out of bed and stumbled towards the bathroom. I was on four hours of sleep and wasn't looking forward to preparing breakfast burritos and potato salad for affluent country club golfers. The only advantage about being at work that early was that I was off at noon.

I turned over the Corolla a couple times before it started then began the twenty-minute drive to Amy's house in southwest Littleton. The sun began to rise on the eastern horizon and it was creating a rose and violet glow through the clouds of the slightly overcast morning. I turned off the radio, rolled down the window, and inhaled the summer air. The drive on C-470 ran parallel to the Rocky Mountain foothills, and I was the only car within sight. It was picturesque and I could not have felt more tranquil, but that quickly changed.

Amy's house was at the end of an eight-house cul-de-sac, and as I turned onto her street, my stomach dropped. I stopped in the middle of the road and stared at her driveway with the blinker clicking and the engine idling. Ken's Volkswagen Golf was parked in the middle of the driveway.

"Fuck," I said, tapping the steering wheel uneasily.

Amy and I had our relationship problems, but nothing I considered out of the ordinary for a couple in their early twenties who enjoyed drinking and debauchery. I could not envision a scenario with her cheating on me, and she knew I was dropping off her car in the morning. She couldn't be that careless.

I felt guilty for immediately assuming that Amy was being unfaithful. Maybe Ken got too drunk at Old Chicago and Amy had to drive his car and he crashed on the couch, maybe Abby had car troubles, maybe Abby got pulled over and got a DUI, maybe the three of them went to Amy's to continue the party.

I pulled the Corolla into the driveway and parked behind the Golf.

I got out of the car and hesitantly walked up to the front door. I was unsure if I should walk in, knock, or ring the doorbell. I surveyed the porch and nothing looked amiss. I was positive that I was overreacting to the circumstances. I knocked softly then leaned against the vinyl siding.

"One-one-thousand, two-one-thousand, three-one-thousand."

I knocked again, this time a little harder and louder. Nothing. I decided to go inside. I slowly turned the doorknob clockwise, and was surprised that the door was unlocked. I turned back to the street one last time then quietly pushed the door open and tiptoed inside.

I was about to call for Amy when I looked down the hallway and froze. Chills rushed throughout my body then I went numb—my fingers, my hands, arms, legs, and feet.

Lying on the hardwood floor about five feet in front of me was an assortment of clothes scattered in the hallway. There was a T-shirt, two pairs of pants, a bra, a pair of boxers, and a pair of flip-flops. I walked closer and recognized the shirt Amy wore the previous night. They must have stripped naked the moment they walked in the house, and practically fucked in the hallway.

I began to tremble and braced my hands on my knees. I simultaneously felt like throwing up and crying. I wanted to curse out Amy, and I really wanted to beat the living shit out of Ken.

I don't know how long I was there, but at some point I stood straight up, took a deep breath, and turned towards the front door. I reached into my pocket and dropped Amy's keys on the floor then walked out of the house, quietly closing the door behind me.

I began the walk to work alone, and heartbroken. I puked twice, once behind an evergreen shrub and once into a metal trash can. On the second occurrence someone peered at me from behind the curtains of a bay window at me. I offered a courtesy wave with vomit dripping from my chin.

I arrived at work and prepared myself for what I imagined to be the longest six-hour shift of my life. I clocked in, washed my hands, and tied a white kitchen apron around my waist.

Three hours into my shift, I was so engrossed in making hundreds of turkey and ham sandwiches that I temporarily forgot about the events that had transpired that morning.

A bartender jarred me back into reality. "Hey Scott, Amy is on line one!" she yelled into the kitchen.

I immediately got sick to my stomach and thought I was going to vomit again, but after a few dry heaves the sensation passed. I did my best attempt at composing myself then began the walk to the phone, and the inevitable end of our relationship.

"Hello," I said in a muted tone.

"Hey sunshine! How's work?"

I paused, realizing she didn't know that I knew that she cheated on me.

"Did you forget that you were supposed to drive me to work this morning?" I said.

"I . . . I . . ."

"I dropped off your car at your house."

"You did?"

"Yes, and I saw Ken's car in the driveway."

She was quiet for a long time and I could faintly hear her start to whimper. I was waiting for a response and willing to have a standoff until she spoke.

"Let me explain."

"I'd love to hear your explanation."

"I slept in my room and he slept on the couch downstairs."

"Don't fucking lie to me! I saw all your clothes in the hallway!"

"I don't. I can't. I'm so sorry."

"Fuck off! Don't ever talk to me again!" I yelled into the receiver as I slammed the phone down.

I felt strangely satisfied until I looked up at the clock and realized she was scheduled to be at work an hour later.

Two weeks later I was walking with Cameron in the gravel parking lot of the Adams County Fairgrounds. I glanced down at the VIP laminate around my neck.

"This is pretty fucking amazing," I said as I flicked the laminate.

"Yeah, it doesn't get much better than this," Cameron responded.

"Technically, it would be better if we were playing on the main stage in front of thousands and had free booze and groupies waiting for us after the set."

"True."

We arrived at the front gate, flashed our laminates to the security guards, and started walking towards the giant inflatable schedule with the list of stages and set times for every band.

The fairground was organized chaos. There were countless crew members and roadies unloading semi-trucks, building stages, performing sound checks, propping up merchandise tents, food tents, drink tents, first-aid tents, and anything else that was required for a festival of 10,000 people. Everyone working looked rather calm considering the show was five hundred miles to the west in Salt Lake City, Utah the previous night and the gates were opening in less than two hours.

"There we are," Cameron said, pointing to a spot on the inflatable schedule.

"We play at noon? What time are fucking doors?"

"I am pretty sure they're at noon."

"Fuck, I need a beer."

One hour and four Bud Lights later I was standing on the portable stage of a twenty-foot semi-truck. The side of the truck opened up to unveil a stage, speakers, stage lighting, music equipment, PA equipment, and had an awning. The stage was backlined, meaning the guitar amps, speaker cabinets and drum kit were provided, and the only equipment required were guitars, instrument cables, and drumsticks. This was to minimize set time changes between bands, and maximize the total number of bands playing on the stage.

"You guys have from 12:00 to 12:30. Thirty-minutes and not a minute over, or we'll turn off the PA," a sound guy told Cameron, Doug, and me.

"Don't worry about us. We'll be under the thirty," I quickly assured him.

"Have a good show."

About ten minutes before noon I looked back to the few hundred people at the main entrance waiting for the doors to open. If half of them came straight to our stage we would have a massive crowd.

The schedule was in our favor because the Warped Tour usually had multiple bands playing simultaneously on different stages, but from 12:00 to 12:15 we were the only band playing. If people wanted to see a band, they had to come to our stage. Not in our favor was the location of the stage. It was about two football fields from the main gate, and if concertgoers wanted to check the schedule, visit the merchandise tents, or grab a beer they'd probably miss us.

"Doors are officially open and you can start whenever you are ready," the sound guy said through the monitor speakers.

I looked at the main gate then the grass field between the stage and the sound booth, there wasn't a single person. Then I looked at Cameron and Doug and shrugged.

"Let's fucking do this," Cameron said as he started playing the chords of our opening song. I closed my eyes and joined in with the bass line.

Our set consisted of seven original songs that totaled a tad over twenty-eight minutes. This left us little time for crowd interaction between songs, and we began the next song while the notes were still ringing out from the previous one. I don't even recall announcing our band name.

"Thanks for watching! This is going to be our last song," Cameron announced to the crowd, which had increased to over a hundred people.

I looked out into the crowd and recognized about fifteen friends and acquaintances scattered throughout the grass field. I searched for Amy but she wasn't there. I was expecting her to show, even though on the surface I despised her, I was still in love with her and missed her. We had been talking sporadically since the infidelity, but we both knew the damage had been done and there was no going back. This was the first show she had missed since we began dating, and it truly signaled the end of our two-and-a-half-year relationship.

"Thanks so much! Please come say hi after we . . ." Cameron said into the microphone as it was turned off and the band on the adjacent stage began playing.

Californication

(Or Chapter 6)

December 2002 – January 2003

It was sometime after 9:00 p.m. on a December night and I was sitting in the middle bench seat of a van I had named "Old Blue." It looked like it had rolled off the assembly line sometime in the late 1970s, and the once-vibrant blue paint had faded from years in the harsh Colorado climate.

The band was driving west on I-80 somewhere between Lake Tahoe and Reno during a heavy snowstorm. The interstate was pitch-dark except for the van's headlights, and the snow reflected the headlights, decreasing visibility to virtually nothing. Periodically, we passed a highway sign that was unreadable because it was plastered with snow.

From time to time Old Blue slid viciously across several lanes after hitting a patch of black ice, but Cameron would quickly correct the slide. Each time it occurred my heart sank, and I white-knuckled the middle console. I came to terms with the fact that a patch of ice could cause the van to crash through the guardrail and careen over the embankment. Accordingly, I repositioned in my seat and unfastened my seatbelt. I would normally be anxious about not wearing a seatbelt, but I concluded being thrown from the vehicle would offer the best chance for survival.

Doug was sitting shotgun and grinning with excitement on every treacherous turn. It was probably due to the handful of mushrooms he ate at a gas station outside of Sacramento. He insisted on listening to Radiohead's *Kid A,* and after some objection from me, he won. The music put me in a trance and I felt like I was tripping by association.

The heater was broken, and our answer to that was to bring a pile of blankets. The blankets offered little benefit that night because the temperature was in the low teens. I was wrapped in three blankets and still shivering, barely able to feel my extremities, and watched as a cold-breath cloud formed on every exhale.

We were driving back to Colorado from a weekend tour that would tally a round-trip drive time of thirty-nine hours and 2,600 miles in a little over three days. I was exhausted and just wanted to sleep, but I was worried Cameron would fall asleep if I wasn't awake to make sure he stayed awake. I stared straight ahead, focusing on the pavement and attempting to look for black ice. I watched the barely visible highway lines zoom by like an endless series of shooting stars.

The tour had started three days earlier. The first leg of the trip was from Denver to Park City, Utah, a five hundred mile jaunt that takes about seven-and-a-half-hours. The itinerary had us arriving in Park City around 4:00 p.m., eating dinner then arriving at the venue sometime around 6:00 p.m. for load-in.

We left Denver sometime around dawn. The first five hours of the drive were uneventful, and we ran on schedule. But about ten miles west of Rock Springs, Wyoming, the first snowflake

71

landed on the windshield, and within minutes we were driving directly into an impending snow storm. The storm was mild by Wyoming winter standards, and it shouldn't have had any effect on our drive, but the front windshield wipers began to malfunction and eventually stopped operating altogether.

We had to reduce our speed due to the limited visibility, and made an unscheduled detour at the next available rest stop. We all jumped out of Old Blue, and began examining the broken wipers. Our mechanical expertise was limited, and after a few minutes we concluded the motor was broken.

"What the fuck are we going to do?" I asked.

"I think we'll be fine. The storm doesn't look that bad," Cameron said.

"Maybe we should try to fix it in the next town," Doug said.

"Fuck that. I'll just drive a little slower and be more cautious," Cameron replied as he climbed into the driver's seat.

I stared at the dirt-and-grease-covered engine that had a corroded battery and duct tape around various hoses.

"Let's go! We're falling behind schedule," Cameron yelled.

I looked back to the darkening clouds then slammed the hood and climbed into Old Blue.

"Those clouds don't look bad. I bet we have at least a few hours before the heavy stuff starts coming down," Cameron said as he pulled the gear shift into drive.

Twenty-minutes later, snow was falling so heavily Cameron had to roll down the window and steer with his head partially out of the van to get an unobstructed view of the interstate. Ten minutes after that, he dumped half a bottle of windshield-wiper fluid onto the window and attempted to wipe it with a clump of Taco Bell napkins, all while steering with one hand and exceeding the speed limit in near-whiteout conditions.

"Maybe we should pull over until this passes," Doug offered.

"No, I'm good."

Five minutes after that, the snow ceased and the sun broke through the clouds. We drove the remaining two hundred miles under clear skies in a little under three hours and arrived in Salt Lake City around 4:30 p.m.

We drove directly to an Advance Auto Parts, pulled into a parking spot and congregated at the front of the van. The three of us stared helplessly at the wipers.

"My guess is the motor is toast." Cameron said.

"Fuck, I barely know how to change oil so your guess is as good as mine," I said.

We walked into the store and approached the clerk behind the counter. He had oil stains on his hands and shirt. We explained our situation, and he stared at us for a moment then spoke. "Did you guys check the fuse?"

"No. No we did not," I responded.

"I would suggest starting there."

"Thanks," said Cameron, his back turned. He was already walking toward the exit.

I rummaged through the glove box until I found a replacement fuse and handed it to Cameron. He removed the existing fuse, inserted the new one, turned the ignition, and put the wiper on its lowest setting. I watched in anticipation.

After seconds of silence, there was a high-pitched squeaking sound of the wiper blades moving across the windshield. It was a minor victory, and minor victories are vital for any tour.

We had two hours until our set. Idle time in an unfamiliar town on a limited budget usually only presented three options: exploring, sleeping, or drinking. The temperature was in the low teens, and I wasn't adequately dressed for the harsh winter conditions, so exploring wasn't an option. I didn't want to spend any additional time in the frozen icebox that was Old Blue, so sleeping wasn't a choice either. That left drinking.

I leaned back into the cheap vinyl cushion of the barstool, inserted five dollars into a bar-top video game, and started playing trivia while sipping on a Coors Light.

Cameron sat next to me. I barely took my eyes off the video game to acknowledge him.

"We have to play two one-and-a-half-hour sets," he said.

"Correct me if I'm wrong, but don't we only have an hour and forty-five minutes' worth of material, maybe two hours if we're lucky?"

"That sounds about right."

"So we're an hour short?"

"Don't worry about it. We'll play some of the same songs in both sets, jam out on a few others, and I'll do a couple covers by myself."

I momentarily contemplated our predicament, then welcomed the musical challenge of improvising sixty-minutes of music. It also helped that I knew if we didn't play the entire three-hour set we might not get paid, and that would result in use of personal money for gas, the hotel, and other band expenditures.

"Sounds good," I said as I raised my pint glass.

Five beers and forty-minutes later I was on stage playing the verse to Rage Against the Machine's "Killing in the Name" on a continuous loop.

"I'm ready whenever you guys are," the sound guy said through the monitors.

"You guys good?" Cameron asked.

Doug and I both nodded, then Cameron started playing our first song without offering any introduction. Not that it was necessary, because there wasn't a single person on the dance floor. The venue was separated into two rooms: the bar side and the stage side. On the bar side there were about fifty people, and on the stage side it was empty.

By the last chord of the first song there were about ten people on the dance floor, and as our set progressed, the crowd steadily increased until there were about forty people watching us. I anticipated that we would play for ten, maybe twenty people if we were lucky. Sometimes when you play in a new town the only people in the audience are the sound guy and the bartender. It happens to almost every band, and it's just something you have to prepare yourself for. I was pleasantly surprised by the turnout.

We extended songs that were a few minutes and stretched them out to over ten minutes. Reggae is ideal for improvisation. Doug and I played a simple, tight rhythm while Cameron freestyled the vocals and added the occasional guitar solo. The crowd loved it and probably thought it was all rehearsed, but we were pulling it out of our ass to increase our set time.

At the conclusion of the first set, I jumped off stage and proceeded straight to the bar.

"Can I get a Coors Light and a shot of Cuervo?"

"Sure thing," the bartender responded.

As I waited, an attractive girl approached the bar and sat two stools to my left. She ordered a few cocktails and joined me in waiting. I casually made eye contact and smiled but didn't drag things out long enough to make the situation uncomfortable.

"How's your evening?" I finally asked.

"Good, just having a little celebration."

"What are you celebrating?"

"Me and a couple friends graduated a few weeks ago and this is our last hurrah together."

"Congratulations!"

For the next thirty-minutes we talked and drank—and she flirted with me like I was the only guy in the room. I don't remember her name, but I'm 70 percent sure it was Amber. She had perfect posture and a petite figure, and was wearing a tight black shirt that accentuated her perfectly shaped breasts. She would have definitely been out of my league in Denver, but I felt an ideal situation in play. I was a touring musician and she wanted one last fling before she returned home to Seattle to begin graduate school. I suspected she wanted a memory, not me—and I was fine with that.

"We're about to go back on. Are you going to come watch us?"

"I'll be there," she quickly responded.

The second set consisted of thirteen songs and had two repeats from the first set and two covers: a very, very extended version of "Stir It Up" by Bob Marley and a reggae rendition of "Patience" by Guns N' Roses.

After we finished the last song I turned off my amplifier, leaned my guitar against the speaker cabinet, and jumped off the stage to join Amber at the bar. She had a beer waiting for me when I arrived.

"That was so much fun! You guys are great," she said, putting her hand on my thigh.

"You don't have to lie."

"I'm not. I promise."

"I'm just joking. Cheers."

We raised our glasses, clinked them together and drank. Then, for the first time all night, there was an awkward silence. We both stared at each other then looked away. A few moments later we both started talking at the same time, and then quickly stopped.

"Sorry, you go," she said.

"Sorry. What were you going to say?" I asked, almost echoing her apology.

We both smiled, and nervously laughed.

"So, what are you guys doing after this?" Amber finally asked.

"I really don't have a clue. There was some talk about driving straight to California, but I'm not sure."

"We're having a little party at the house, and I think you guys should come."

"Yeah—that sounds cool to me."

I was dumbfounded. A beautiful woman was hitting on me because I played in a band. This is something every guy dreams of when they start playing an instrument, and I had never prepared myself for the moment.

"Do you have to ask the rest of the band if they want to go?"

"Yeah, I probably should ask them."

I prepared myself for the dismount off the barstool and focused on the landing because I did not want to fall, or trip, or do anything that would be embarrassing. I carefully stepped off the stool and placed both feet squarely on the tile then nonchalantly walked towards the stage. Once I was out of view, I began a full sprint. I jumped onto the stage and almost fell face-first into the bass drum after tripping on an instrument cable.

After I gathered my balance, I stood in front of Cameron and placed my hands on his shoulders. I had an ear-to-ear smile. I composed myself then said, "So that group of girls asked if we wanted to go to their house for a party."

"I don't think so."

"Wait? Did you say you don't think so?"

"It's almost one," he said, looking at his phone. "And it's going to take like another hour to break down the equipment and get the van loaded."

"Okay, we'll load out as fast as humanly possible and get to the house around two. I don't think they are going to bed anytime soon."

After a short pause, Cameron responded: "I actually just want to drive to Cali right now. I'm sober and wide awake and don't really feel like a party."

"Are you fucking with me?"

"No."

"I need to hear this again. Are you fucking kidding me?"

"It's like a twelve-hour drive and I don't want to start it in the morning with everyone being hungover."

"A group of hot girls is asking us to party and you're worried about us being hungover? I could care less if one of us is puking out of the van on the highway. This is a once-in-a-lifetime opportunity."

"It just sounds like a bad idea. I'm going to finish loading the van, go get paid, and we're going to head out."

"You would rather spend the night in the van?"

Cameron thought about the question then nodded.

"Fuck you," I said. I turned around and walked away.

I returned to Amber and explained the conversation with Cameron. She looked perplexed. "I guess—it kind of makes sense."

"It doesn't, and I have no idea what he's thinking. Sorry."

"Don't be sorry, I had fun tonight."

"Me too, and for what it's worth you're a pretty awesome girl."

"Thanks! So I'm thinking about heading out to Denver this summer. We should exchange emails and meet up if I make it out there," Amber said. She wrote her email address on a bar napkin.

"I'll definitely write you when I get home."

I wrote my email on a napkin then slid it across the bar and took the napkin with her email and stuffed it into my pocket, knowing I would probably never talk to her again.

We hugged and said goodbye. Thirty-minutes later I was back in Old Blue driving west on I-80 towards California and the Pacific coastline.

I awoke on the stain-covered carpet of Old Blue with hardened drool on my cheek and sunlight peering into my eyes. My head was pounding, my teeth chattered, I was dehydrated, and I had to pee. I wiped drool onto my hoodie.

The van was quiet except for the hum of the engine and a talk radio station that was at such a low volume it was barely audible. I wanted to go back to sleep, but the constant vibrations of the van as it went over the highway bumps made it almost impossible. After a few minutes I pulled myself up onto the middle bucket seat and slowly opened my eyes to survey the surroundings.

Outside the van the countryside was desolate, and there wasn't an exit or building in sight. This was not a place you would want to run out of gas. I was unsure of how far we had driven, the Sierra Nevada Mountains in the distance were the only indication that we were going in the accurate direction. Cameron was driving, but barely. He looked exhausted after having driven the entire night. Doug was passed out in the passenger seat with his head and neck against the window at an angle that looked about as uncomfortable as I could imagine.

"Where are we?" I asked, clearing my throat.

"About an hour outside of Reno."

"Any rest stops coming up?"

"I don't know."

I was about to ask a follow-up question, but it sounded like Cameron didn't want to make any unplanned stops so I leaned back into the seat and attempted to close my eyes.

We crossed the California state line, then drove through Sacramento, San Jose, and arrived in Santa Cruz sometime that afternoon. It was over twelve hours of driving. The only stops had been for gas and the occasional bathroom break.

We were scheduled to play that evening at an 800-capacity venue called the Catalyst. We were opening for two local Santa Cruz bands, the Expendables and the Lonely Kings. When the Expendables had come to Denver we added them to one of our shows, so they were returning the favor. The Denver show with the Expendables happened the same night as a late-spring blizzard that brought over eight inches of snow and essentially shut down the city. Minus the bands, bartender, and sound guy, I counted a total of seven people in the audience. This show wasn't going to have the same fate as the Denver show because it had sold-out the previous day.

When I walked onto the stage the venue was packed, and I realized it was the largest show I had ever played. I didn't know a single person in the audience, and it was unnerving to look down at hundreds of strangers packed onto the floor and up against the stage and knowing the vast majority of them had never heard any of our songs.

After the first song I knew we had won the crowd over, and by the end of the half-hour set the crowd was so loud it felt like we were playing in front of thousands. The Expendables were hands-down a better band, but we held our own, and I was proud of that. At the merchandise table I was asked to take pictures and sign autographs, my first rockstar moment outside of Colorado.

Six hours later, I was standing in the lobby of the Santa Cruz Hampton Inn. Cameron and Doug were in our room on the verge of passing out, but I was still in the midst of a euphoric high. I was about to explore the streets of Santa Cruz when I noticed a girl working the front desk. She looked bored, so I decided I would strike up a conversation with her rather than walking aimlessly on the wet, cold night.

I arrived at the counter and she looked up from the computer screen.

"Hi! How can I help you tonight?" she asked in a bubbly tone.

She was chubby, but cute. The top two buttons of her blouse were undone, exposing her enormous cleavage. I had a perfect vantage point from the counter, and we were both aware that I was staring at it, but neither of us cared. Her name badge read "Claire."

"Hi Claire, how's your evening?"

"I'm great! How can I help you tonight?" she responded with a smile.

"Nothing really, I just saw you sitting here and thought I would come over and chat."

"Oh, that's a first."

"I'm sorry, if you don't feel like talking I can leave."

"No, you're fine. It just hasn't happened to me before," she said, starting to blush.

"That's strange. How long have you worked here?"

"Let's see. I moved here in September and started a few weeks later."

"Where are you from?"

When intoxicated, I sometimes ask a lot of rapid-fire questions, Twenty Questions–style.

"Tulsa, Oklahoma."

"That's a pretty big move. Why Santa Cruz?"

"Do you really want to know?"

"That's why I asked."

"Well—I wrote five cities on a piece of paper then tore them apart and put them into a hat. I closed my eyes and pulled out a piece. It said Santa Cruz, so I moved here."

"Are you serious?"

She nodded.

"You didn't know anyone here?" I asked.

"Not here, but I have a cousin in San Francisco."

"That's crazy. I could never do anything like that."

"Why not?"

"I don't know."

"I feel like you can't be afraid to try new things and live to the fullest. If you hold back, you might regret something."

We continued talking for another five minutes until a guest approached the lobby. I slowly backed away from the counter then walked out the front entrance. I briefly stood on the sidewalk then pulled my coat over my head to form an improvised shelter and started walking towards the sound of the crashing ocean waves.

Ten days later, I was awakened by my phone vibrating on the nightstand. I grabbed it and squinted at the screen with one eye. It was Cameron.

"Why the fuck are you calling at seven in the morning?"

"I'm quitting."

"Huh? Quitting what?"

"The band. Your equipment is on your porch."

I instantly sprung out of bed, thinking I misheard him.

"What do you mean you're quitting? What about the shows we have booked?"

"I'm canceling them. I'll explain it later. Good luck." He hung up before I could respond.

I ran out of my bedroom wearing only a T-shirt and a pair of boxers. I swung open the patio door and on the cement floor was my musical equipment.

"Fuck! Fuck!"

In the coming weeks, I came to discover two things about Cameron's call that morning:

1. The shows were not canceled.

2. He lied to me. He didn't quit the band, but had been practicing with my replacement for weeks without my knowledge. He essentially fired me from the band but decided it would be easier to covertly drop off my equipment and make an early-morning phone call than fire me face-to-face.

I was pissed, and felt betrayed. I'd almost prefer reliving Amy's infidelity than getting kicked out of another band. Almost.

I never learned the true reason why I was kicked out, and I really didn't care to know. I surmised I had fallen out of favor with the band and they needed new blood, out with the old, in with the new. It was my Pete Best moment.

Less than three years after I was kicked out, they played Red Rocks Amphitheatre in front of a few thousand people. The show was for an event called Film on the Rocks that happens every summer and pairs a Denver band with an iconic movie. They opened up for *Ferris Bueller's Day Off.* I was not in attendance.

...And Out Come the Wolves

(Or Chapter 7)

February 2004 – April 2004

Band Number Three
Genre: Punk rock
Influences: Rancid, Bad Religion, Descendents, Pennywise, and NOFX
Members: David—vocals; Rich—guitars, backing vocals; Sam—guitars, backing vocals; Greg—drums

I auditioned for Band Number Three sometime in January of 2004, after the replacement for the band's original bass player abruptly quit. The audition took place in a dimly lit basement across from a laundry room in a house in the affluent suburb of Highlands Ranch, Colorado. The two-story middle-class house was a stark contrast to the guys in the band, who were the definition of punk. They looked like they hadn't showered in days and were wearing shirts that seemed like they hadn't been washed in weeks, which was ironic considering they practiced ten feet from a washer and dryer. I had a suspicion they were squatting in the house.

Greg and Sam had started the band while in high school and recruited David, Rich, and a bass player to complete the lineup. They began playing shows in the college town of Fort Collins, and after a few years they made a band decision to move south to Denver. I met the band for the first time sometime in 2000, when they played a house party hosted by Band Number One. There was trash-talking between the bands and a brawl almost broke out in the kitchen.

I arrived at the audition without knowing any of their songs. Not a single note. I sat down and opened a Mead notebook then sketched a crude image of a guitar. I scribbled down fret numbers and corresponding strings as Rich taught me three songs on the spot while the rest of the band waited impatiently. After thirty-minutes I was ready.

We played the three songs continuously for the next three hours. During the final hour I was playing virtually mistake-free. I was confident about my performance, and my only concern was that I played the bass with my fingers instead of using a pick. Playing with a pick allows for increased speed and stamina, but playing with your fingers allows for better control and more dexterity. When I began playing bass I decided on the latter approach and never properly learned how to play with a pick. I felt like I was at a disadvantage, because punk songs usually have a fast tempo and the majority of punk bass players use a pick.

I felt they were apprehensive about my playing style. The communication between us was minimal, which led me to wonder if they were extremely serious musicians or assholes, or if they remembered the near-brawl in the crowded kitchen.

"We'll be in touch," Rich said as I packed my gear.

I didn't hear from them until two months later when Rich called out of the blue.

"What do you think about coming to the studio and recording "Down and Out" for us?" he asked.

"I think I remember that one. When?"

"Tomorrow."

"Fuck, how much time would I have?"

"A couple hours."

"That should be plenty of time."

"Cool, I'll call you in the morning with the address."

I was actually unsure if I could record the song in the allotted time because I didn't remember it. I opened the Mead notebook, hoping I didn't tear out my notes after what I thought was a failed audition. Towards the back I located the tablature. I stared at it, and then I slowly started to remember the song. After a few minutes I was moving my finger across the paper while humming the music.

I spent the rest of the evening practicing the three-minute song: intro, verse, chorus, verse, chorus, bridge, and chorus, over and over and over again. I practiced until I memorized the song and I could play it with my eyes closed.

I arrived at the studio sometime after ten the next morning. I had a brief conversation with the band and the recording engineer, then I was ushered into the sound booth. I was exhausted, a little hungover and alone. The heavy, soundproof ten-foot-by-ten-foot room was virtually silent, and I thought I heard my heart beating. I slid on the headphones and awaited instructions.

"Let me know when you're ready," the engineer said through the headphones.

"I think I'm good to go."

"Do you want to run through it a few times or do you just want to jump right in and record?"

"Let's just fucking record it."

"Okay. I'll start with the click track and then the guitar will come in."

A click track is a beep that's played along with the music to assist the musician. It ensures the recording maintains the same tempo, with no speeding up or slowing down. It's a necessity for any professional recording.

I gave a convincing thumbs-up to him and the rest of the band who were in the control room behind the glass. I felt like everybody was taking bets on how badly I would fail and how many takes I would need to complete the song. I guessed the over/under was set at seven.

The click track slowly faded in and I began to tap my foot to the rhythm of the click. I placed my index and middle finger on the E string, concentrated on the click, and awaited my cue to begin.

Three minutes and twenty-five seconds later the guitars and cymbals started to fade out. I carefully removed my fingers from the strings so I wouldn't produce any unwanted sounds. I immediately looked up to the control room and attempted to gauge my performance.

"What did you guys think?" I asked.

"It sounded good, really good," someone said through the intercom.

"I think you nailed it," said someone else.

"Could you play it back so I can give it a listen?" I said.

I took off my bass and sat against the carpeted wall. I adjusted the headphones then placed a hand over each ear pad, lowered my head, and listened meticulously. I felt confident after the first listen, but asked for it to be played again. After the second listen I was convinced that I recorded the entire song mistake-free. I stood up and looked into the control room. I could see that everyone was talking, but the intercom was turned off so I was deaf to the conversation.

"I'm really fucking happy about that take," I said.

"You got it. Nice work," the engineer responded.

Two days later I was invited to join the band.

Smash

(Or Chapter 8)

June 2004 – May 2005

Three months later I was staring out the window of a Chevrolet Sportvan driving south on I-25 en route to Las Cruces, New Mexico. The band was traveling through the night to reach Las Cruces by 8:00 a.m. and begin the first of fourteen dates on the Warped Tour. We weren't an official band, or a band that would even be playing on a stage or inside the gates. Our plan was to find a location outside the main entrance of each venue, set up a makeshift stage and play for the crowd that was waiting in line to enter the show. We were essentially crashing the tour.

"We'll get to play for everyone going into Warped Tour. It'll be thousands! I bet more people will see us than a lot of the bands actually on the tour," Rich said when he proposed the idea to me.

I wasn't as convinced. I was unsure how staff and security guards would feel about an entire band setting up their drums, guitar amps, bass amp, and PA system on private property without prior approval. I thought we would get greeted with a "Get the fuck out of there" or, better yet, "You assholes are trespassing and we're calling the cops." I tried not to think about those scenarios.

I stretched out on the middle bench seat of the van, which I had personally named "the Green Monster." Rich was driving, Greg sat shotgun, and David, Sam, Kim, and Beth were in the back playing cards. Kim and Beth were "merch girls" who had the job of selling CDs, T-shirts and any other band merchandise that would make a dollar. They were doing the rock 'n' roll internship for free in exchange for a summer experience of touring with a punk band across half the country.

I was the greenhorn in the band, and within the first few hours of the drive I could tell these guys had been friends and bandmates for years. I felt like an outsider. I was the hired gun, a replacement of a replacement.

I turned on the dome light and looked at the tour itinerary.

Warped Tour 2004

June

Tue 6/29 Las Cruces, NM - N.M.S.U. Practice Field
Wed 6/30 Peoria, AZ - Peoria Sports Complex

July

Thur 7/1, Fullerton, CA - Cal State Fullerton
Fri 7/2, Fullerton, CA - Cal State Fullerton
Sat 7/3, San Francisco, CA - Pier 30/32
Sun 7/4, Las Vegas, NV - Desert Breeze Skate Park
Tue 7/6, Chula Vista, CA - Coors Amphitheatre
Wed, 7/7 Ventura, CA - Seaside Park
Thur 7/8, Wheatland, CA - Sleep Train Amphitheatre Lot
Fri 7/9, Boise, ID - Idaho Center Amphitheatre Lot
Sat 7/10, George, WA - Gorge Amphitheatre Lot
Sun 7/11, Saint Helens, OR - Columbia Meadows
Tue 7/13, Vancouver, BC - Thunderbird Stadium
Thur 7/15, Calgary, AB - Race City Speedway
Fri 7/16, Bozeman, MT - Gallatin County Fairgrounds

Sat 7/17, Salt Lake City, UT - Utah State Fairgrounds
Sun 7/18, Denver, CO - Mile High Stadium

The total distance was approximately 5,400 miles through eleven states, with an estimated drive time of fifty-two hours. It was almost equivalent to driving from Los Angeles to New York and back—and we were planning to do it in a van with over 150,000 miles and no working air conditioner. We'd be doing it, though, alongside some of the best punk bands in the world, including Bad Religion, Avenged Sevenfold, My Chemical Romance, Flogging Molly, New Found Glory, NOFX, Rise Against, Taking Back Sunday, Atmosphere, and Yellowcard, to name drop a few.

The band made the decision to skip the San Francisco show because driving from Los Angeles to San Francisco to Las Vegas was an additional 950 miles and fourteen hours, so driving straight to Las Vegas would save us 650 miles, ten hours of driving, and seventy dollars' worth of gas. It would also give us an additional night in Vegas. We also planned to skip the Canada shows, but this had nothing to do with gas mileage or drive time, it was because Sam had a felony, and felons aren't permitted entry into Canada unless they receive special permission from the Canadian government.

Behind the Green Monster was a six-foot cargo trailer that was at full capacity with four electric guitars, two acoustic guitars, one bass guitar, two Marshall guitar amps and cabinets, a Mesa boogie amp, an Ampeg amp and 8x10 cabinet, a full PA system, a five-piece drum set along with the hardware, cymbals, and cases, an assortment of guitar pedals, replacement strings, drum heads, drumsticks, guitar picks, and any other miscellaneous musical items that were required for a twenty day tour.

Each of us had one suitcase, and mine contained three print T-shirts, three band T-shirts, four pairs of Dickies shorts, one black hoodie, five white Hanes T-shirts, five pairs of boxers, six pairs of black ankle socks, two toothbrushes, three extra pairs of contact lenses, two twenty-four count boxes of citrus-scented Wet Ones, and an assortment of other toiletries.

There were also numerous totes of band merchandise including CDs, T-shirts from extra-small to XXXL and hundreds of band stickers. The merchandise was essential because it would be our only source of income after the band fund was depleted.

The band account only contained a few hundred dollars, and if we didn't sell merchandise that account would deplete rapidly. That worried me because I didn't want to use my personal money for band expenses. For the foreseeable future I planned to live off a $1,200 insurance check that I received after a hail storm totaled my 1998 Volkswagen Passat. That was all the money I had to my name, and I had to save $700 for rent when I returned. I didn't even have a credit card in case of an emergency. I don't think anyone did.

At the time, a gallon of gas averaged $2.03. The van averaged about eighteen miles per gallon, and the trip would require three hundred gallons. Using those calculations, the total gas cost would be approximately $609. Our only other band expense was five nights of hotel rooms: two nights in Las Vegas, one night in Irvine, California, and one night in downtown Portland, Oregon. The rooms essentially doubled the band expenditures.

During the nights we didn't have a hotel room we planned to drive and sleep in shifts. If everyone was too tired to drive, we would crash in a wide assortment of parking lots: Warped Tour venue parking lots, Wal-Mart parking lots, gas station parking lots, rest area parking lots, and, occasionally, more scenic parking lots inside city and state parks.

I knew if the van encountered any mechanical issues and needed repairs we were going to be in a jam. We could afford to replace a tire or a dead battery, but anything beyond that we were going to be fucked.

Jake's new band was officially scheduled to play the entire Warped Tour for the second consecutive year, and while driving from Dallas to San Antonio Jake ran over an errant ladder that punctured all four tires and almost caused the band's van to roll over. The four replacement tires and the tow cost them almost $1,000. This accident happened on day four of a fifty-six day tour. If we encountered fate like that, our tour would be finished and I would be taking a Greyhound back to Denver.

Day 1, Las Cruces, New Mexico

We arrived at the New Mexico State University campus around 7:00 a.m., and after driving around in vain for ten minutes we finally located the N.M.S.U. practice field.

"Let's go see where we can start setting up," Rich said as he jumped out of the van. Sam and Greg followed.

I walked in the opposite direction, towards the parking lot with a never-ending stretch of tour buses, vans, and trailers with license plates from states all over the country. After ten minutes I spotted a van with Colorado license plates and as I approached Jake exited the passenger door. I began sprinting towards him.

"What the fuck is going on?" I said as we hugged.

"Fucking exhausted. We drove through the night and I'm on a few hours of sleep."

"Do you want to go grab a coffee?" I asked.

"I can't. I have to start unloading these fucking trucks, and I'm already late."

Jake's band was playing the entire tour, but there was a catch. They had agreed to work as roadies in exchange for their spot. Every day they had to work five to eight hours of manual labor for the opportunity to play a thirty-minute set. It was grueling, but an amazing break for an unsigned band, and one that could not be passed up.

"Already?"

"Yeah, but we'll catch up soon."

"Cool, have a good show."

"You too."

I resumed my journey through the parking lot and returned to the Green Monster about thirty-minutes after I had departed. Greg was setting up his drums under a pop-up tent about a hundred feet from the main entrance and the soon-to-be concert line.

"That looks pretty far. Do you think we should be closer?" I asked Rich.

"I don't want to get too close to the main gates."

"I guess we'll just have to play really fucking loud."

We spent the next hour trekking gear between the van and the stage. The drums were placed under the tent on a drum rug, which sat on uneven ground. The guitar amps were on both sides of the drum kit and the PA speakers were on speaker stands outside of the tent. Three mics, mic stands and two monitors with their cables strewn across the grass field were in front of the tent.

We powered up the generator, turned on the amps and PA, and performed a quick soundcheck. We were ready to play, but the crowd was not. There were less than thirty people in line.

"I guess we're a little early," I said. I decided to take refuge in the back of the van from the already scorching New Mexico sun.

About twenty-minutes later I emerged from the van and the crowd had increased to a few hundred people. It was show time. I was moments away from the start of the first song of my first show with the band and collectively our first show on Warped Tour. I was confident. Hot, but confident. The temperature was in the mid-nineties and there were beads of sweat rushing down my forehead, which I wiped with the back of my hand.

Sam picked the first notes and was quickly joined by Rich playing the same notes but at a different octave. Greg entered with a slow snare drum roll that rapidly increased. There was a brief pause then the guitars, drums and bass commenced like a sonic boom. The song blared across the field. At the start of the first verse David began the vocals. During the second verse I almost did the splits on the grass but regained my balance before tumbling to the ground.

At the conclusion of the first song about 20 percent of the crowd applauded, while the remaining 80 percent completely ignored us. I was ecstatic with the reaction of the 20 percent and for the first time since leaving Denver, I was excited about the potential of the tour. As we continued to play, the applause gradually increased.

The gates opened about twenty-minutes into our set and the line started to move as people entered the field. As the line progressed, we played to a new segment of concertgoers waiting to enter the main gates, creating a new audience about every fifteen minutes. This cycle went on for about the next two hours until the line finally started to diminish.

At the conclusion of this marathon set my face was bright red and my black T-shirt was completely drenched. I looked like I had just climbed out of a swimming pool. We had played our forty-minute set four times essentially back-to-back-to-back-to-back with only a few minutes' in-between each set, and in near-triple-digit temperature. It was the longest and hottest set I had ever played and I was convinced one of us was going to pass out from heat exhaustion.

I wanted to sit in front of an air conditioner pointed directly at my face for hours, but that wasn't a possibility so I staggered to the van and pulled a Pabst Blue Ribbon out of the cooler and placed it against my forehead. After a few minutes I opened the beer and slammed it, then lay down and closed my eyes.

We spent the rest of the day breaking down the stage, loading the van, drinking beer, and listening to bands perform from the grass field outside the main gates. The Green Monster left Las

Cruces around 10:00 p.m. and began the five-and-a-half-hour drive on I-10 towards Phoenix. I passed out ten minutes after departure, partially from exhaustion and partially from the booze.

Day 3, Fullerton, California

The tour was two shows down, twelve to go when we headed to Fullerton, a city about forty-minutes southeast of Los Angeles and known for being the birthplace of the electric guitar.

I had visited the greater Los Angeles area once before when I was eighteen. I ended up in Hollywood and the infamous Sunset Strip. I was awestruck with the Hollywood sign and I remember thinking this is where dreams are made. Then I glanced to my left and saw a homeless guy defecating in an alley. It felt appropriate. For every dream achieved, thousands are broken and dissolve into nothing.

I continued west on Hollywood Boulevard past high-end restaurants, porn stores, souvenir shops, and homeless shelters with million dollar-houses on the hillside as a backdrop. I stopped on the corner of Sunset Boulevard and Clark Street in front of the famous Whisky a Go Go. It was the club that launched the musical careers of Guns N' Roses, Mötley Crüe, Van Halen, System of a Down, and Linkin Park, to name just a few of the globally famous bands that played there.

"I'll play here one day," I said to myself. "I guess I should probably learn how to play first."

Not only did I learn how to play, but I returned to California in a band that was touring in the parking lot of Warped Tour. I had not fulfilled my promise of playing the Whisky stage, but I felt it was something that was attainable, and that was something I would have never thought possible when I was standing on the corner of Sunset and Clark six years ago.

After we finished our set on the second day in Fullerton we constructed a plan to sneak into the tour. We knew that every day hundreds of musicians and crew members as well as countless managers, merchandise staff, photographers, journalists, food vendors, volunteers, and general staff gained access using a variety of different backstage laminates, badges, passes, and tickets. We didn't have any credentials, but we concluded that as long as we walked in with confidence the security guards would assume we were just one of the hundred bands that were playing that day. Using a couple of empty guitar cases, drumsticks, and a microphone as decoys, we casually strolled past the security guards and through the backstage entrance.

The plan went off without incident. Once inside, we hid our musical decoys behind a food tent along the fence line then joined the thousands of ticket holders for a day of punk rock music. That was the first and last show we had to sneak into. Eventually, we formed friendships with some of the roadies and they offered us backstage passes in exchange for work at the end of the day. We quickly agreed to the arrangement, knowing that if we did hours of hard labor it would get us one step closer to playing inside on an actual stage. It was our attempt at replicating Jake's band's strategy.

Later that night we celebrated the accomplishment of playing our first four shows by getting drunk in the parking lot of the Cal State Fullerton campus. I drank, got drunk and passed out with a PBR in my grasp. The next morning, I awoke to the musk of five guys and two girls who hadn't showered in five days. I escaped the stench of the Green Monster and did an imitation shower with hand wipes that I rubbed on my arms and legs, masking my body odor with a fresh lemon scent. I pissed behind a palm tree, brushed my teeth with a-half-empty PBR, and did a morning stretch routine. I felt like I was prepared to make the journey across the desert to Las Vegas.

We began the five-hour, 270-mile drive around 9:30 a.m. I wanted to start earlier, but coordinating seven people who had drank until dawn is never an easy task.

We were on I-15 outside of Baker, California, when the temperature became unbearable. It was noon on July 3 and we were driving through the desert in a van without a working air conditioner. The temperature gauge was so far in the red-hot zone that I thought the needle was going to break off. And since the van was on the verge of overheating, we had to turn the heater on high, a counterintuitive but effective way to cool an engine.

We were driving 80 mph with the heater on high and the windows down through one of the hottest locations in the world at high noon in the middle of the summer. I have never been to the sun, but I cannot imagine it being much hotter than what I experienced on that five-hour drive.

We stopped for gas in Baker, home to the World's Tallest Thermometer. The last thing I needed was a reminder that it was close to 110-degrees, but I stood in front of the hundred-foot thermometer. The hottest temperature ever recorded on Earth occurred about an hour north of this town, and these assholes built a statue to heatstroke. I wanted to spit on it but opted to conserve my saliva.

We got back onto I-15 East towards Las Vegas, driving adjacent to the Mojave National Preserve, commonly known as the Mojave Desert. Heat distortion radiated off the black asphalt surface, which was sprinkled with skid marks that ran off into gravel embankments. An occasional exit sign or emergency call box appeared on the horizon. The unforgiving desert backdrop extended for miles in either direction, and only adaptive vegetation that could survive the harsh climate, like prickly pear, brittlebush, and California Juniper, was visible.

I slithered into the faux-leather chair and embraced the face-melting wind as sweat escaped every orifice of my body.

Day 5, Las Vegas, Nevada

We arrived in Las Vegas that afternoon and promptly drove straight to our hotel, an off-the-strip La Quinta Inn. Rich checked in, then each of us covertly snuck into the room with suitcase in hand. The room was small and not intended for seven adults. The two queen beds were claimed by the time I reached the room, and I resigned myself to the fact that I would be sleeping on the pesto-colored carpet.

One by one everyone took a shower, with my place in line being fourth out of seven. By the time I showered the hot water was gone, and it felt like I was bathing in a frozen lake. The temperature ultimately had little effect, and I proceeded to take one of the longest and most refreshing showers of my life. I wouldn't have the opportunity to shower again for seven days.

After everyone showered, we discussed how to spend our first night in Las Vegas. Rich, Greg, Kim, and Beth were exhausted and chose to stay in the room. They opted for TV, pizza, and a functioning air conditioning unit. David and Sam decided on booze and gambling on the Vegas Strip. I opted to join them. I was exhausted, but knew I would have numerous opportunities for sleep. I only had that one night for debauchery on the Strip.

Within an hour I was separated from David and Sam, and I was content with that. I had been in the company of the band for something around 120 hours, and was looking forward to time to myself.

I walked on the strip with a Bud Light tallboy in hand, making my way through tourists, gamblers, street performers, and prostitutes. I walked past a flabby middle-aged guy with a bad comb-over devouring a double-scoop ice cream cone that had stained his beige button-down shirt. He was oblivious to everyone else on the strip and didn't have a care in the world. I hoped one day I'd reach that same level of not giving a fuck about what other people think.

My journey on the Strip took me past the Bellagio, Caesars Palace, the Mirage, and Treasure Island. I drank and walked for hours until I finally stumbled into the Riviera. I walked through the brightly lit and cigarette smoke-filled casino floor, past endless rows of slot machines, craps tables, roulette tables, and various blackjack and poker tables.

I decided to sit at a nickel slot machine and inserted a five-dollar bill, then watched the machine light up with 100 credits. I was among a sea of degenerate gamblers hypnotized by the colors and sounds, yearning for the next spin to be the big winning jackpot. An hour later, I was down forty dollars and all I had to show for it was two free ten-ounce Bud Light drafts served in a plastic cup.

I exchanged smiles with an elderly lady sitting two machines away. She had been chain smoking and relentlessly pressing buttons the entire duration of my failed gambling experience.

"How are you doing?" she asked as she ashed her cigarette into the ashtray between our machines.

"Not so well," I responded, pointing to my remaining credits. She resumed playing.

"It only takes one credit to win the jackpot."

"I guess you're right."

I played the final five credits and lost.

"Good luck," I said as I got off the stool, but she didn't hear me. She was laser-focused on the liberty bells, numbers, and fruit symbols, blocking out everything except the animated screen a few inches from her face.

I contemplated her claim, and I realized I had the same mind-set towards my prospects of becoming a full-time musician. It only takes the right person to hear a song and love it, I had told myself. At that moment I felt I had as good of a chance of becoming a rockstar as her winning the jackpot.

I saw a bank of payphones and made a beeline directly to them. I grabbed a receiver, dialed zero to make a collect call, and then slowly slid my back down against the carpeted walls until I was on the floor. I knew my friend Mark was having a house party that night and a majority of my friends were going to be there. I was supposed to be there. I missed home, I missed my friends, and I missed my family. Don't get me wrong, I liked the guys in my band, but they felt more like coworkers than friends. The band felt like a job, and I needed to hear familiar voices. I spent the next two hours talking to different people at the party. It was comforting to hear them, and it boosted my morale.

I made the two-mile walk back to the hotel and was utterly exhausted by the time I arrived at the room, well exhausted and drunk. I grabbed a towel from the bathroom, balled it up to use as a pillow, and located an open spot on the floor in front of the bathroom doorway and fell asleep. The next morning I awoke to someone almost tripping over me on their way to the bathroom.

Day 9, Ventura, California

Our shows had been exceeding my expectations, but the Las Vegas one was the most successful in terms of audience size, crowd reaction, and merchandise sales. Maybe it was due to the Fourth of July, or maybe everyone was delirious from the triple-digit temperature, or maybe we were just starting to sound really good.

After Las Vegas we played another successful show in Chula Vista, on the US/Mexico border. Then we left town and drove north up I-5 to the 101 then west towards Ventura and Seaside Park.

The band was hitting its stride with stage location selection, setup, sound, and overall music performance. I felt confident that rumors of our parking-lot performances had reached Warped Tour management and it would only be a matter of time before we were invited to play on a stage within the perimeter fences. I would soon remember that an inflated level of self-confidence can be dangerous for a musician.

That confidence started to wane at the Seaside Park show. Thirty seconds into our first song I broke the E string, and had to decide if I was going to continue playing, finishing the song on the remaining three strings, or abruptly stop mid-song to replace the string. I decided to finish the song. The results were not good.

Once the song was finished, I unplugged my bass and ran behind the tent while the rest of the band continued the set. I located my guitar case and pulled out a replacement string, and within ninety seconds I had removed the broken string, placed the new string through the bridge and around the tuning post, and tightened the string around the post. I tuned the new string and rejoined the band prior to the start of the third song.

My bass had four strings again, but the new string kept falling out of tune, and on some songs it sounded like I was playing the wrong notes. I had to re-tune after each song to ensure the string remained in tune. That was the first musical hurdle I faced that day.

The second hurdle was my amplifier. It was cutting out for seconds at a time, resulting in no sound from the speakers. I ensured all the cables were fully plugged in and adjusted a few different knobs, but the problem persisted. I came within seconds of shoving the amplifier off the cabinet. That, combined with the out of tune string, made it sound like I was a novice bass player. It was the worst set I had played in years.

After our last set we loaded the trailer, and I walked out of Seaside Park towards the sidewalk that runs parallel with the Pacific Ocean. The sound of the waves crashing onto the shoreline was incredibly tranquil and I momentarily forgot about my disastrous performance. I continued, walking towards Ventura Pier and the sound of a girl singing and playing guitar.

She was probably in her early twenties, playing a beat-up electric guitar and singing through a small amp. There was a bucket in front of her with a piece of paper taped to it that said "Tips for my Music Career."

I leaned against the wood railing and watched the water beneath me as she sang "Sweet Child o' Mine" by Guns N' Roses and "Time after Time" by Cyndi Lauper. She was good, really good. She possessed natural talent and I was getting chills watching her play. It always amazed me that you can hear incredible musicians playing anywhere there is a potential audience, including a beach boardwalk. This girl deserved a bigger stage than tourists on a pier. I walked over and dropped two dollars in the bucket and she smiled.

"Good luck," I said as I walked away. "Hope yours is better than mine."

Day 10, Wheatland, California

The next morning I was uncomfortably awoken by sunlight in my eyes and the unbearable morning temperature inside the van. I reached for the nearest item in an attempt to shade my face, but it was in vain. The personal sun blocker I grabbed was a dirty T-shirt with the stench of stale beer combined with body odor. I threw it into the back of the van as fast as I grabbed it. I knew that with the smell, sunlight, and temperature I wasn't going back to sleep.

I sat up on the passenger seat, rubbed my eyes, and adjusted my clothing. When I adjusted my shorts, I felt something odd, but I was unsure what had happened. I first suspected that I fell asleep with a beer in my hand and it slipped into my lap when I passed out. I touched my crotch to confirm this, but that wasn't it. My next suspicion was that I pissed myself, but that wasn't it either. Then it hit me.

"Fuck," I said.

I turned around to survey the van and make sure everyone was still asleep. With this confirmed, I slid my hand into my shorts. My last presumption was correct: I'd had a wet dream. I was almost thirty and hadn't had one since I was in my early teens. I wasn't sure if I should be embarrassed or proud.

I exited the Green Monster and walked aimlessly until I located a convenience store. I grabbed the key attached to a wooden stick from the attendant and went into the bathroom. I removed my shorts and boxers, threw the boxers into the trash can, and stared at myself in the mirror. I was haggard. My patchy beard was growing in, my complexion was discolored, my face was oily, and large dark circles under my eyes had the appearance that I hadn't slept in days.

I spat in the filth-stained sink then placed both hands onto it and stood there for a long time. In the reflection I noticed graffiti on a bathroom wall that was soliciting takers interested in "a good time."

Over the next eight days we played four shows in four states, driving from California to Idaho through Oregon onto Washington, then back to Oregon, back through Washington and Idaho, then onto Montana. We slept where we ended up. One night it was in a room at the Hampton Inn in Portland, and another we slept in the van while parked in Coeur d'Alene National Forest.

Day 17, Butte, Montana

We were in Big Sky country, broke and hungry. Cash had dwindled and meals had become scarce. We had been surviving on gas station food and Taco Bell since California, and we even went to a Spokane soup kitchen but they were closed.

The van was parked in a gas station parking lot adjacent to a Pizza Hut. The aroma was so overwhelming I could taste the pepperoni in the air.

"Let me see if I can do some bartering for food," Greg said, and jumped out of the van.

I watched intently as he strolled across the parking lot and entered the circa 1970s-style Pizza Hut. Five minutes later he walked out with a smile from ear to ear.

"I got us some fucking pizzas."

"Are you fucking kidding me?" I responded.

"I offered them ten CDs and five shirts in exchange for six large pizzas."

"That's fucking amazing!" Rich said.

My mouth began to salivate and I victoriously punched the air.

"Where's the merch? I want to do this deal before they change their mind."

Greg grabbed a handful of CDs and five T-shirts then exited the van with both hands full. After a long wait he walked out of Pizza Hut carrying six pizza boxes that towered to his chin. We ate like kings that evening, and the next morning.

Day 19, Salt Lake City, Utah

I was walking through the gravel parking lot of the Utah State Fairgrounds when I looked up and saw Kevin Lyman walking in my direction. Kevin was the founder of Warped Tour, one of the tour's producers, and the person that oversaw the selection of all the bands that played. He was the bigwig, and if he liked your band, chances were good that he would find a stage for you to play on.

As he approached I timidly gave a courtesy wave then looked toward the tour buses parked beyond him.

"Do you play in the band that's been playing in front of the main gate?" Kevin asked.

"I do," I said as I cleared my throat.

"I like what you guys have been doing."

"Thank you."

"Are you guys planning on doing the entire tour?"

"No. We're from Denver—so tomorrow is our last day."

He paused. "Tomorrow is pretty full, but let me see if I can get you guys on a stage since it's your hometown."

"That would be amazing. Thank you so much."

"Take this and go grab dinner," he said as he opened his wallet and handed me a crisp hundred-dollar bill.

Day 20, Denver, Colorado

When I looked up and saw mile marker 299 next to the "Welcome to Colorful Colorado" sign, I realized I was home. I had driven past the Colorado welcome sign more times than I can remember, but I vividly remember seeing it on this drive. It had been almost three weeks since I left the confines of the state, and I was happy to finally be home.

I arrived at my apartment sometime after midnight. I stood in the hallway contemplating my first action home: eat, shower, or sleep. I decided on eating, but since I hadn't been home in three weeks my food options were limited. I put a frozen burrito in the microwave and watched the display until it reached zero. I took the plate with the burrito and walked to the couch and turned on the TV.

I wanted to stay on the couch and sleep for forty-eight hours, but I had to be awake at 8:00 a.m. to drive the van to Mile High Stadium and begin setting up for the final show of the tour. I began watching a rerun of *Saturday Night Live* and was asleep before the monologue finished.

I arrived at Mile High Stadium a little after 9:30 a.m., and the rest of the band was already there waiting for me, the van, and the equipment. I had been around these four guys for almost every waking moment for twenty straight days, so I was rather unexcited to see their faces again.

As I began unloading our equipment I was optimistic that one of Kevin Lyman's assistants would come to our tent and inform us that we were playing inside. An hour before our parking-lot set my optimism had diminished, but I was still holding out hope for a last-minute invitation. Ten minutes before our set I knew our invite wasn't going to happen. For whatever reason, we were destined to be the band that played in the parking lot.

Still, I consider our Denver show the best one of the tour. The sound was great, we played mistake-free, and it had the largest and most enthusiastic crowd. It helped that there were friendly faces in the audience. I counted at least twenty people I knew in the sea of a few hundred.

I continued playing with the band for another year, but I abruptly quit in May of 2005. They had just announced their plans to play the parking lot for the entire two months of the 2005 Warped Tour: forty-eight dates spread over fifty-nine days in twenty-six states and four provinces.

At the time I wasn't exactly sure why I quit, but looking back I realize my heart wasn't in the music, and I could no longer fake it. I loved playing, but I didn't love the music and I wasn't having fun, so I walked away. They had less than three weeks to find my replacement.

About a month into the tour, their van rolled over somewhere on the East Coast after the driver fell asleep. No one was seriously hurt, but the van was totaled and the band had to cancel the rest of the tour.

Jake's band also played that tour, from start to finish, and as it progressed so did their popularity. At the Denver show they were invited to play the main stage.

"You have to be on stage when we play," Jake told me.

"If you can get me onstage, I'll be there."

"Don't worry about that. I'll get you up there."

They were given a 2:30 p.m. set time, and when they walked onto the stage the crowd numbered in the thousands. I stood behind Jake's drum set and watched their entire half-hour set in awe. I can't say I wasn't envious, but I couldn't think of anyone more deserving.

The moment their set was finished, I walked up to Jake and hugged him from behind. "I'm so fucking proud of you," I said.

In the following years Jake's band had two songs included in the direct-to-video movie *American Pie Presents: Band Camp*, completed five consecutive years of playing every Warped Tour date, had their songs played on MTV shows, and won multiple Best Band in Denver awards from local publications and radio stations. Jake even had a bass drum head included in a special Warped Tour exhibit at the Rock and Roll Hall of Fame.

Jake had reached 72 percent rockstar, and I was once again without a band.

Grassroots

(Or Chapter 9)

May 2007 – June 2007

I was sitting at a dive bar on Broadway Avenue in central Denver with some friends when I glanced over at a guy inserting dollar bills into a digital jukebox. His uncombed grey hair was receding well beyond his forehead, and his face was thin and weary. He typed into the keyboard on the touchscreen until he located the song he was looking for, pressed play, and dejectedly returned to his stool at the bar and resumed drinking alone.

He stared blankly into the half-empty pint glass, and waited patiently for his song to begin. His only movements were lifting the glass from the bar top to his mouth and motioning to the bartender for another drink.

"Don't Stop Believin'" by Journey ended and the bar went silent. Then the opening guitar riff from "You Shook Me All Night Long" by AC/DC echoed throughout the tiny bar. At the sound of this, the man's head sprung up with a smile from ear to ear, he was a changed man. He went from depressed to exuberant in four short bars of music, all because of a simple rock song. He started playing air guitar then switched to drumming on an invisible snare drum and hi-hat, then back to the guitar.

At the conclusion of the three-minute-and-thirty-second song, there was a short pause and drunken conversations could be heard again. Then, as abruptly as it ended, the same AC/DC guitar riff rang out and he resumed the air performance all over again, this time with even more passion.

After the third time I anticipated the guitar of Angus Young to play yet again, but instead "SexyBack" by Justin Timberlake blasted over the speakers. The man's head dropped, and he looked defeated. The ten minutes of happiness and memories vanished, and he transformed back to his pre-AC/DC demeanor.

Music has a way of evoking memories from the past, and songs are forever linked to family, friends, relationship, times, and locations. It's the time stamp of life: the good, the bad, the sad, the happy, the tragic, and the amazing.

I vividly remember the first time I heard *Mellon Collie and the Infinite Sadness* by the Smashing Pumpkins. I was nineteen and it was October of 1995. I was sitting in my Ford Ranger next to my girlfriend in a parking lot overlooking Denver. I slipped the first disc into the CD player and we listened to the entire double album with minimal conversation while staring out to the city lights below us. Every time I hear a song off that album, I am instantly transported back to that night.

Whenever I hear "Smells Like Teen Spirit" by Nirvana, my memories go back to high school and hearing a sound I'd never heard before. Whenever I hear "Comfortably Numb" by Pink Floyd, I remember being at Mile High Stadium for my first concert and, along with 76,000 other fans, watching Pink Floyd perform a flawless three-hour set. Whenever I hear "Wonderwall" by Oasis, I remember my first love. And whenever I hear "When September Ends" by Green Day, I remember being at a funeral for a friend who died too young.

About twenty-minutes after the AC/DC songs ended my friends and I paid our tab. While we were walking out of the bar, I made a detour to the jukebox. I inserted five dollars into the machine and selected "You Shook Me All Night Long" to play three more times.

I continued to play in various insignificant Denver bands, going through the cycle of auditioning, joining, and quitting usually within a six-month period. Since I quit Band Number Three, I did this with four different bands over the course of two years. I wanted to play music, but I didn't want to play music that someone else wrote.

My first problem was I didn't know how to play guitar, and writing songs on bass can be difficult. The list of songs initially written on bass guitar is very short. Another problem was that I couldn't sing, and that made it difficult to write lyrics and melodies. And to be honest, my lyrics were mediocre at best. I felt they were closer to nursery rhymes than rock 'n' roll anthems.

I was at a musical crossroad when my phone rang. It was Mark. I'd known Mark for over a decade and played shows with his band countless times. He played guitar and sang lead vocals in a hard rock band that was a combination of Chevelle and Helmet.

After a brief conversation, Mark asked, "Do you want to come to Nebraska and play a few shows with us?"

"What about Rob?"

"He has to work or go to a wedding or some other shit and can't."

I thought about it for five seconds then said, "I'm fucking down."

Mark's band had booked a weekend tour that consisted of three shows. Two of them were on Friday in Lincoln, Nebraska, at a venue called Knickerbockers, and the last one was the following night in Kearney, Nebraska, at an Italian restaurant that doubled as a venue on the weekends. The Friday night event consisted of an early show that was all-ages, and a late show that was eighteen and over.

"Do you think you can learn the set in two practices?"

"Yeah, I think so."

After I hung up I inserted their disc into my CD player, and started to play along with their songs. I knew if I wanted to succeed I'd have to spend a lot of time learning their songs on my own, because this band didn't like to practice. They liked to play shows, drink, party, and do their best attempt to portray the rockstar lifestyle—once destroying a Westin hotel room and getting banned from the hotel chain. These activities left minimal time for practice.

I wasn't thrilled that I'd only have a few hours of practice with Mark and Jim, the drummer, but there were three factors in my favor:

1. I was an extremely fast learner. I had the ability to remember notes after playing them just a few times. I attribute this to my numerous auditions and aptitude with numbers.

2. The songs were simple. Most of them had a verse-chorus-verse-chorus-bridge-chorus structure, so once I learned the verse and chorus I knew 90 percent of the song.

3. I had seen them play countless times, so I had a solid comprehension of their music.

"That sounded great," Mark said at the conclusion of the second practice.

I wasn't so confident. I left Jim's house after that practice, drove to 7-11, purchased a large coffee, and practiced with the CD until 3:00 a.m. My alarm was set for 5:15 a.m., and we were scheduled to leave town at 6:00 a.m.

We left Denver in Jim's Jeep Liberty with a four-by-eight-foot U-Haul cargo trailer containing our music equipment and suitcases. Jim was driving, Mark was in the passenger seat with a bag of sunflower seeds in his lap, Max was behind Mark, and I was behind Jim. Max was the roadie, guitar tech, drum tech, driver, merchandise person, and anything else that we would need on the trip.

We got delayed thirty-minutes by the morning rush-hour traffic, but once we were outside city limits the congestion eased, the speed increased, and the drive on I-76 to the eastern plains of Colorado became dreadfully boring. The scenery was nothing but grass fields, farming fields, weeds and dirt—lots and lots of dirt. Once in a while, there was a herd of cows.

We drove past towns with names like Brush, Crook, Ovid, and Julesburg, and the further east we drove, the more barren the landscape became. This is the part of the country where families go to birthday dinners at a Subway or Arby's attached to a gas station.

"It would fucking suck to live out here," Mark said while he spit sunflower seeds out the window.

I nodded then looked at the tour itinerary in my notebook.

Nebraska Tour - June '07
Denver to Lincoln: 7 hours/488 miles
Lincoln to Kearney: 2 hours/133 miles
Kearney to Denver: 5 hours/360 miles
Total Trip: 14 hours/981 miles

We passed the Nebraska border a little over three hours into the drive, and from there it was a four-hour drive due east to Lincoln, the state capital of the Cornhusker State. Until this writing I didn't know what a cornhusker was, apparently it's either a person or machine that removes the husk from a corncob, or slang for a person who enjoys stimulating an uncircumcised penis.

For the rest of the drive I did a combination of two things: sleep and stare out the window at the vast empty nothing.

We arrived in Lincoln around 4:00 p.m. and parked in front of Knickerbockers. The venue wasn't open yet, so we did the logical thing and walked to the closest bar to commence drinking.

"Cheers buddy, thanks for filling in for us," Mark said.

I really wanted to play sober, or at least as close to sober as possible, but this band enjoyed drinking—and more importantly, enjoyed drinking while playing. To their credit, they could pull it off remarkably well, some bands performed worse when they were drunk, but this band excelled. I knew I was about to embark on a forty-hour drinking adventure, so I picked up the beer and clinked glasses with everyone.

"Let's fucking rock it tonight," Jim said.

"Salute everyone!" Mark said.

We drank heavily for the next two hours, and by my count I had five beers. I had a moderate buzz, which I didn't realize until I got dizzy from standing up too quickly.

We walked back to Knickerbockers, loaded in, and performed a quick soundcheck. When we finished I then proceeded straight to the bar and patiently waited for the surly bartender. He was preoccupied with cleaning pint glasses. The bottles on the shelves behind him were covered in dust and looked like they hadn't been touched in years.

I rotated my stool 180-degrees and took in the surroundings. There were numerous guitars hanging against the brick facade and framed pictures of bands that had performed there. Most of them I had never heard of, and by judging from their hair and makeup a lot of them looked like they were from the 80s hair-band scene. There was a poorly designed flyer advertising "35¢ Taco Tuesdays" in the front window.

The bartender finally approached me. He had all the charm of a debt collector.

"Hey, how are you?" I said.

"What can I get for you?"

"Do bands get anything free?"

"Two pitchers of beer."

"Okay. Can I get a pitcher of Coors Light?"

He turned away without saying another word and began pouring the beer.

I was finishing the final sips of my first beer when the doors opened and people, mostly teenagers, began entering the dimly lit room and spread sporadically across the dance floor. The venue had a capacity of about 300 people, and five minutes before showtime I could count almost everyone in the audience.

The first band started at six, and we began a little after seven. There were about thirty people scattered throughout the venue when I walked onstage, and at the end of our forty-minute set the crowd had almost doubled. By the time the headliner went on the audience had grown to over a hundred people.

The headliner was a band from Omaha I'd seen on numerous occasions in Denver, and I was unsure why they weren't signed to a label and a recording contract. I still consider them one of the best unsigned bands I ever played with or saw. They had two front men who had amazing voices and could shred on guitar with the best of them, and their songs were complex, catchy, and entertaining at the same time, a feat that's extremely difficult to pull off.

The first show ended, and the venue promptly kicked everyone out and began letting in people for the second show. We opened that show to about a hundred people and by the end of the night there was barely room to stand on the dance floor. The door guy probably violated fire code by admitting people beyond maximum occupancy.

I watched the headliner from the back of the venue and began critiquing my performance. I had counted four minor mistakes, and those were probably mistakes only musicians would catch. They were stuff like coming in a little early for a chorus or playing the incorrect note but instantly correcting it. Unless you had a musician's ear, they were essentially nonexistent.

We celebrated the show by taking a shot of Jäger—and then repeated this celebration again and again and again and again. I can't remember the official count, but between the four of us I estimated that we drank eight pitchers of Coors Light and probably half a bottle of Jägermeister. By the end of the show I was nearly blacked out and unsure if I needed water, fast food, or an alley to pass out in.

I stumbled from the bar to the merchandise table and carefully positioned myself against the wall, placing both palms on it as support. I concentrated on standing upright. I didn't want to collapse face-first into the table or a potential customer.

Out of one of my remaining open eyes I saw two women approach the merchandise table and strike up a conversation with Mark and Jim. They purchased two CDs and asked for our autographs. Mark and Jim signed the CD insert and handed it to me, and then I scribbled an illegible signature with a black sharpie and handed it back to Jim. I resumed focusing on standing upright.

"What are you guys doing after the show?" one of the girls asked.

"I don't know. No plans, really," Mark said.

"You guys want to come party at our house?"

That grabbed my attention because I knew what they were insinuating. Mark and Jim knew as well, and it would have been a no-brainer, but they both were overweight, on the other side of forty, and—if I am being honest—not very attractive. We briefly contemplated the invitation, but in the end we went to a Taco Bell drive-thru, purchased twenty dollars' worth of tacos, then went back to the hotel room and passed out.

I awoke the next morning to a repeat of a College Softball World Series game on ESPN. I went into the bathroom and rubbed my fire-red eyes. I stared into the mirror and couldn't decide if I looked worse, or felt worse.

"Fuck," I muttered.

I knew if I stopped drinking the hangover would commence, and I wanted to avoid that at all costs. With this goal in mind, I walked to the lobby and poured a glass of orange juice and a bowl of Fruit Loops from the free continental breakfast area and returned to the room. I sat at the edge of the bed eating cereal while drinking brass monkeys and watching softball.

"Who's winning?" Mark asked.

"Does it matter?"

"The girls on Arizona are pretty hot."

"Yes—yes they are."

Mark and Jim began drinking breakfast beers, and within an hour all of us had become so engrossed in the game that we developed a rooting interest in the Arizona Wildcats. At the conclusion of the Wildcats victory we left the hotel and made the short two-hour drive west on I-80 from Lincoln to Kearney.

Upon arrival in Kearney, we checked into the Hampton Inn, put our bags in the room, and spent the next four hours walking the streets of downtown Kearney, visiting numerous bars while continuing to watch the College Softball World Series.

Sometime around 6:30 p.m. we arrived at the venue that doubled as a local Italian restaurant, or more accurately, the restaurant doubled as a music venue. The promoter approached our trailer as we were unloading and introduced himself. He had a green mohawk and wore a leather jacket with band patches sewn onto it.

"Hey guys, I'm Puke and I want to say thanks for playing tonight," he said.

"Your name is Puke?" Mark asked.

"It was a nickname that stuck."

"Well nice to meet you--Puke." Mark said as he shook his hand. "We're just wondering if there are going to be people eating dinner while we're playing?"

"No, the stage is on the other side of the dining room,"

"Isn't the noise going to bother them?"

"No, it's fine. I book shows here every weekend."

"And people still come here to eat?" I asked.

"Best Italian in town."

We took the stage a little after eight, and started the first song while families were still enjoying their lasagna, eggplant parmesan, and chicken alfredo in the adjoining room. It was the worst show of the weekend. All three of us made mistakes, and judging by the crowd's reaction they heard each one of them. One kid intensely stared at me with his arms folded during the entire set, not offering a single cheer, clap, or smile. I was irritated at the kid at first, but I realized we sounded horrible, so I didn't fault him for the lack of enthusiasm.

I wanted to blame the performance on the aroma of garlic and marinara sauce, but it was probably due to the fact that the three of us drank continuously for two straight days. It was a weak performance, but we'd played two out of three shows at a high level and I considered that a success, especially since the three of us had only practiced together for a few hours.

The next morning I awoke with a pounding headache and minimal memories of what occurred after our set. I genuinely didn't want to know. I got dressed, left the room and grabbed a muffin on the way out of the hotel, then hobbled to the Jeep. As I fastened the seatbelt I mentally prepared myself for the miserable five-hour drive home. I considered vomiting into a bush in the parking lot before we left. Instead, I rested my head against the window and closed my eyes.

Twenty-minutes later we merged onto I-70 and began the drive west towards Colorado. I stared quietly out the window at the flat, barren grassland that stretched as far as I could see.

My Beautiful Dark Twisted Fantasy
(Or Chapter 10)

June 2008 - October 2009

Band Number Four
Genre: Pop punk and alternative rock
Influences: Green Day, Rise Against, blink-182, and the Offspring
Members: Mark—guitars, vocals; Travis—drums; Justin—guitars

I always promised myself if I didn't "make it" by the time I was thirty-five I was going to stop playing music. I gave myself over a decade to become a rockstar, and if I didn't achieve that status by my thirty-fifth birthday I would hang up the guitars, sell my equipment, and never walk onto a stage again.

I had seen countless guys in their late thirties and early forties who were still holding onto the dream of making it—playing a shitty venue in front of a few-dozen people while still believing that the next song would be their big break. It was sometimes pathetic, sometimes sad, and I didn't want that fate for myself, so I instituted a self-imposed musical expiration date.

Almost all musicians will have a day when they walk off stage and never hear applause again. It might happen when they're twenty-two or forty-two, but unless they beat the odds and have a career like Mick Jagger, Paul McCartney, or Bruce Springsteen, it will come to an unceremonious end. I began to wonder if mine was going to be at an Italian restaurant in a backwoods town in Nebraska.

I was broke, living paycheck to paycheck, and routinely went negative in my bank account. Electricity and car payments were past due, and student loan payments were completely ignored. I could barely afford food for my ten-pound dog. It was the life of a struggling musician, and it was not how I had envisioned the start of my thirties. Maybe it was time to get a grown-up job, start a family, buy a house, and become an adult, but I was scared that I'd wake up one day in my sixties and realize I worked a menial job in an endless sea of cubicles counting every remaining minute and hour, because I gave up on my dream to follow the safe path. Giving up on a dream is hard, but realizing when it is time to give up is harder.

"One more year, I promise," I said to my dog as he stared at me in confusion.

I picked up an acoustic guitar, a pen, and a notebook. I had ideas I had been playing around with for years, and I thought they had some potential of becoming a song. I wanted to write them on guitar, but never bothered to learn. I figured it was time to change that.

I sat in silence for a long time then started strumming an A-power chord over and over—and over—and over again until my fingers were numb. I took my hand off the strings and saw that my index and pinky finger were bright red and had formed deep indentations. Over the years my fingertips had formed calluses from bass strings, but since I wasn't playing regularly the calluses had somewhat diminished. Also, guitar strings have a smaller, thinner gauge than my fingers were used too, and they produced a somewhat unpleasant feeling. I continued playing until a blister exploded, dripping blood onto the body of the guitar.

I practiced for the next few weeks, slowly adding more notes and rhythm into the mix. I gradually constructed a rudimentary but complete song.

After two months I had put together the structure of three songs, and decided to invite Mark over for a Saturday afternoon jam session. His band—the one I was a fill-in bass player for—had dissolved after eight years, and for the first time in fifteen years he was band-less.

Mark had started playing guitar and singing in his early teens, and by high school his punk band had elevated themselves to one of the best punk bands in Denver, opening for national acts like blink-182, MxPx, Goldfinger, and Unwritten Law. Mark had toured the country playing music before he received his high school diploma.

That band built a large fan base throughout Colorado and surrounding states, and they garnered the interest of various independent record labels. One small label offered them a record contract and an advance of $75,000 to cover recording costs, new equipment, and additional expenses. The contract was on the hood of Mark's car ready to be signed when Joe, the lead guitar player, balked.

"I want my dad to look at this," Joe said.

The following day, Joe quit the band and the contract was never signed. Mark reminisced about that story often, and I couldn't imagine how devastating it must have been. Not many people have their dream in their hand, only to have it snatched from their grasp.

I considered Mark a very talented musician, one of the best I had ever played with, but he was also lazy and hated to practice. He relied on natural-born talent, but talent can only take you so far. Lebron James got to the NBA because of talent, but practice and mastering his craft has made him one of the greatest basketball players of all time.

I, on the other hand had zero natural talent, and thus dedicated myself to countless hours of practice. I needed to play songs until they were second nature and I wouldn't have to think about what I was playing. They would become as instinctive as breathing or blinking. This required muscle memory, and that required lots and lots of practice.

Mark arrived at my apartment with a guitar gig bag in one hand and a twelve-pack of Keystone Light in the other. He looked ready to play music and get drunk, and I was hopeful the former happened before the latter. We sat down on the couch, opened a beer, and began tuning our guitars.

"I think I'm good," I said. "You?"

"Yeah. Let's see what you got."

I grabbed a pick, placed my fingers on the fretboard, and incorrectly strummed the first chord. I was nervous. It was the first time someone besides my dog had seen me play guitar.

"Fuck, sorry about that. Let me start again."

Mark nodded at me then drank from his beer. I felt like he was expecting the worst and he was preparing for a long day of listening to an amateur play guitar. I lowered my head and restarted the song. About halfway through the second verse, Mark began playing along with decent proficiency.

By the time we reached the second chorus he was playing like he had practiced the song for hours, and not someone who was hearing it for the first time. A good musician has a sixth sense for song structure.

After the song finished I looked up at him to gauge his reaction. He nodded, then reached for his beer and took a big swig.

"I like that. Play it again, I have a couple ideas," he finally said.

One hour later Mark had written the lyrics and the melody for that first song. Three hours, one trip to the liquor store, and fifteen beers after that, we completed a second song and had the formation of a new band. Now we needed a drummer.

My first choice for a drummer was Jake, but he was still playing in his very successful band and probably would have laughed in my face if I asked him. My second choice was my friend Nate. I had attempted to collaborate with him on various musical projects, but nothing ever developed beyond a few practices. Nate was a talented drummer, but he was also a very raw, self-taught one. He hit the drums harder and louder than anyone I had ever seen play, but he was inconsistent and forgetful. He was also married with a kid and had other passions besides music, so I was unsure about his ability to commit to a band. Still, I knew the odds of finding a drummer as talented as him were slim, so we scheduled a practice together. It also helped that Nate lived in a house with a basement that had a large open room perfect for practice—because Mark and I lived in apartments under 900 square feet with neighbors in every direction.

We arrived at Nate's house and set up. Within thirty minutes he had worked out a rudimentary drumbeat for the first song. We proceeded to our second song until he had a rudimentary beat for that one, and then went back to the first song, rotating between the two over the next three hours. By the end of the first practice, Nate had created a solid drumbeat to both songs and I was confident about him being our drummer.

"That sounded good. Really fucking good," I said, looking at Mark.

"So—do you want to join the band?" Mark asked.

"Fuck yeah I do!"

123

Over the next two months we practiced three to four times a week, continually adding to our repertoire of songs. Our intense practice regime had produced six original songs, two cover songs, and one song from Mark's previous band—for a total of nine songs, or roughly thirty-five minutes of music.

"I think we're ready to book a show," Mark announced.

Our first show was on August 16, 2008, at a venue called the Toad Tavern in Littleton, a south-Denver suburb. Located in a rundown strip mall next to a laundromat and liquor store, the place was more of a bar than a music venue, and I would even go out on a limb and call it a dive. It hosted an illegal nightly poker game in the backroom and the happy hours were usually only attended by the local derelicts. It was filthy, bleak, and brimming with the stench of stale beer from the countless beers that had spilled onto the soiled carpet. On a scale of one to ten, I would give it a three.

In other words, it was the perfect venue for our first show. There would be mistakes, and I'd rather them happen at a dive like the Toad Tavern than a venue I respected. Another advantage of playing the Toad was that I lived less than a block away, and I knew I could easily stumble home with my gig bag on my shoulder after a night of drinking.

The show included four other local bands and we were scheduled for the fourth slot. The payout was dependent on how many people came through the door to see us play. We would receive two dollars per audience member, but that would increase to four dollars if we exceeded thirty people. If no one showed, we'd only get two free beers per band member.

"So we only get paid forty dollars if twenty people come?" Mark asked.

"Yeah," I said.

"That's fucking bullshit."

"That's why we need to get fifty people there."

I arrived at the Toad Tavern a little after 7:00 p.m., and after I loaded in my gear I proceeded to the bar for a night of friends, drinking and music. The two opening bands were downright horrible. I mean, they tried, but many local bands either haven't had sufficient practice or just lacked talent, or both. I felt like I was watching a high school talent show, and I sensed the crowd felt the same. After each song there was minimal applause, and whatever was offered felt more like pity clapping. It takes a certain degree of courage to perform original songs, and I respect that. I just didn't want to listen to them. We hadn't even taken the stage and I already knew we were the best band playing that night.

The third band ended unceremoniously, and almost immediately Metallica's "Enter Sandman" blared through the PA speakers in a seemingly attempt to purge the last two hours of amateur music.

"You ready to rock this fucking place?" Mark asked, patting me on the shoulder.

"Let's fucking do it," I replied.

I hopped onto the stage and offered the obligatory praise for the band that just finished, then helped them get their gear off the stage. I turned my amp on, turned up the volume, and played "Seven Nation Army" by the White Stripes as my soundcheck. Minutes before our set the crowd had reassembled on the dance floor, with forty or fifty people standing below me.

"What's up everyone? This is our first fucking show so hopefully you guys like it," Mark said into the microphone.

Thirty-seven minutes later I stood at the edge of the stage as the final note of our final song echoed through the PA speakers. I had one foot on the monitor and pointed my bass to the ceiling triumphantly. The crowd had doubled, and their applause was thunderous. I looked towards Mark and he smiled.

"That was fucking amazing," I mouthed to him.

A few weeks after the show, and right before practice, Nate looked up from his drum set and said, "I have to quit guys, I'm sorry."

"Are you fucking serious?" I asked.

Nate had two passions: playing drums and riding motocross, and his wife had given him an ultimatum that he could play in the band or ride his dirt bike. He decided to quit the band rather than sell the bike. She was also probably upset about us getting drunk and practicing at her house a couple times a week. I couldn't blame her for that.

"I can play the show we have booked but that'll be the last one," he explained.

Five months after our first practice we were without a drummer and a practice spot, and the future of the band was in question.

"Do you want to keep playing?" I asked Mark.

"Are you fucking kidding me? It'll be easy to find a drummer."

I wasn't as confident about the prospect of finding a new drummer as talented as Nate, but I'd already promised myself that this was going to be my last band, and I wasn't going to throw in the towel after mere months. Mark and I began our search for drummer number two.

We rented a practice room in a decrepit building in a run-down neighborhood in South Denver. It wasn't an area where you'd see daily drug deals or convenience store robberies, but it wasn't far off. I brought my guitar home after each practice to minimize the chance it'd get stolen if the room was broken into.

The room cost $175 a month and was five feet by five feet, about the size of a large bathroom. We split the rent 50/50, and at that time my net monthly income was around $1,500, so eighty-eight dollars was a considerable chunk of my pay.

The room could barely accommodate our gear, which included a guitar amp and cabinet, bass amp and cabinet, and four-piece drum set. Mark and I had to stand back-to-back to fit into the room with our equipment. It was a tight squeeze, but it worked and it was only temporary. Our plan was to audition drummers, select the best one out of the group, and move into something larger—something that didn't feel like we were standing on top of each other.

Our search for our next drummer consisted of posting ads on Craigslist, posting on different online music forums, hanging flyers in music stores and asking friends in bands. The results were less than desirable, but we selected who we felt were the four best candidates and scheduled auditions. Two of them were no-shows, one of them was an unemployed guy in his late forties, and the last one arrived at the practice spot with zero equipment. That wasn't a major issue since we had a drum set in the room, but he didn't even bring drumsticks.

"What kind of kit do you have?" I asked.

"It's a black six-piece Mapex set, and it's a fucking beauty. I'm pissed because I had to pawn it for money for a court fine, but if this audition goes well I'll find a way to get it out."

That statement worried me, as I was hoping to find someone without a criminal record, but we proceeded with the audition after locating a pair of drumsticks we found in a hallway trash can.

A top-level drummer is vital to the success of any band. I've played with, and seen hundreds of unsigned bands, and the bands that have real potential always have a very talented drummer. A talented drummer will make subpar musicians sound better, and a subpar drummer will make talented musicians sound worse. I don't care if you have Jimmy Page playing guitar—if you have a horrible drummer the band is going to sound like shit.

Searching for a new band member is an agonizing process and, in some ways, worse than dating. In our case, the prospective member had to meet certain musical prerequisites.

1. Talent: This was far and away the most important prerequisite. If the talent level was phenomenal, the next four prerequisites could be overlooked. Most auditions didn't pass this portion of the test.

2. Age: At thirty-two I felt like I was almost too old to play in a local band, so I didn't want anyone much older than me.

3. Appearance: We were a pop-punk band that wore skater attire, and I didn't want someone with two-foot dreadlocks that looked like they were about to go to a Phish concert.

4. Gear: Professional gear is required to sound like a— professional band.

5. Personality: If they passed the first four prerequisites, they still needed to be someone I would want to hang out with for hours and someone we could tolerate during tours.

Our fourth and final auditionee met none of the prerequisites, and we cordially thanked him for coming and never contacted him again.

Our final show with Nate was again at the Toad Tavern, and moments after our set a girl I didn't know walked up to me while I was standing on the patio.

"Hey," she said.

"Hello."

"My boyfriend is going to be your next drummer."

"Who are you and who's your boyfriend?"

"I'm Travis's girlfriend."

"Okay—who is Travis?"

"Your next drummer."

"Is he any good?"

"He's amazing."

"Well I guess we should give him an audition."

Two weeks later we auditioned Travis, and it was almost immediately apparent that he met the five prerequisites. He was a talented drummer with a very high musical intelligence. He was obtaining a degree in music performance, could read and write music, and had knowledge of music theory. In comparison to Mark and I, he was a musical genius. My only concern was that he had never performed in a band outside of a school setting, but his talent overrode his lack of experience so it was an easy decision to invite him to join the band.

After Travis joined the band I was at a songwriting pinnacle and my creativity was at an all-time high. I was writing song after song after song, about two a week. Some good, some bad, a lot of them were horrible, and most of them didn't leave the confines of my apartment, but I didn't care because my focus was writing music.

I had two black Mead notebooks full of barely legible lyrics and scribbled guitar tablature. Chord progressions and song structure ran adjacent to guitar notes, lines, arrows, underlines, and asterisks that included brief explanations of each song. Once I was confident with each song I'd record rough versions onto my phone as a way to remember the structure and rhythm.

A major shortcoming with my songwriting was I could only write about one central theme: girls. My songs were about relationships, breakups, love, and heartbreak. I didn't know how to write songs about social issues, or politics, or war, or death, or coming-of-age, and every other theme seemed as foreign to me as German. I didn't want to be a phony, so I stuck to what I knew best: relationships and heartbreak. I was a professional in those areas.

The majority of my songs and the lyrics would eventually end up in a trashcan and the recordings would get deleted off my phone forever, but I knew the more I wrote, the better I would become, and the odds of writing a great song would increase significantly.

Shortly after Travis joined the band, we added Justin as a second guitar player. The addition of a second guitar added layers to the music and allowed Mark to stop playing guitar and sing on certain parts of songs. It enhanced the overall sound, made us sound fuller, and made us louder. And louder is always better.

Before our first show as a four-piece we did a band photo shoot in the alley behind the Gothic Theatre. I was satisfied with the outcome because band photos can be disastrous. I blame this on the amount of money bands are willing to spend, which results in usually hiring an inexperienced photographer. Most photo shoots I've done were free because either: the photographer was a fan of the band or they were looking to build up their portfolio. In this instance, you truly get what you pay for, and the results can be some really cringeworthy band photos. There's the cliché shot of everyone standing on train tracks, or walking down an alley with power lines overhead, or every member wearing sunglasses, or matching outfits, or each member looking in different directions, or—my personal favorite—the one with each member holding their respective instrument, just to remind the viewer that this is a picture of a band.

The newly restructured band began playing shows throughout the Denver metro area to decent audiences, and by early 2009 the shows were getting bigger and bigger. To my surprise, we quickly started gathering a following and our fan base grew rapidly. I remember looking down into the audience and seeing people I had never seen before singing the lyrics to our songs. It's an amazing feeling hearing a crowd sing lyrics that were once scribbled into a notebook.

Most of our shows had a party vibe, featuring music, drinking, and debauchery. We mixed music, relationships, work, and nightlife to various degrees of success. I was having the best time of my life playing music, and knew this was the best band I had played in. I was also cognizant that most bands have a very short shelf life. Friends and fans grow up, move away, get married, have kids, and musical interests change and grow. I knew we only had four or five prime years, and I was going to take full advantage of them.

In August of 2009, we emptied the band bank account and booked studio time at The Blasting Room in Fort Collins, Colorado. The Blasting Room is a professional studio operated by first-class producers and engineers, and bands on major record labels have spent tens of thousands of dollars to record there. Rise Against, the Descendents, Black Flag, A Day to Remember, and another fifty or so top-tier punk and alternative bands have recorded there, and some of those sessions have produced gold records that hung in the studio hallways. There wasn't a studio in Colorado that could make us sound as good as The Blasting Room could, and luckily for us it was only a couple hours north of Denver.

The downside of recording at a professional studio was the hefty price tag of $600 a day. We wanted to record a full-length record, but we didn't have the money or time required for it, but it was mostly the money. We decided to record a four-song EP over a weekend.

Our plan was to record drums and bass on day one, and guitars and vocals on day two. Each day came with a ten-hour limit, and I'd be allotted about four hours to record my bass parts. I calculated it would take about an hour to set up and get the correct bass tone and sound. That left me with about forty-five minutes for each song. I wasn't ecstatic about my time restraints, but I knew if I was laser-focused it would be ample time. I was more worried about Travis. This was his first time in a recording studio, and there's always a learning curve in regards to recording.

I sat on a couch and watched Travis and the engineer painstakingly tune each drum. Hit the drum, tune it, hit the drum again, and tune it again. This happened over and over and over again countless times for every drum. I was in a trance of boredom watching them prepare the drum kit, and I alternated between practicing my bass lines and watching the minutes on my cell phone tick away. In the end, it took them almost three hours to set up, tune, and mic his drum kit. We hadn't even pressed record yet and were already down to seven hours.

Once the drums were set up, Travis was incredibly proficient. He completed the four songs in a mere three hours, leaving me with the four hours I had planned for.

I pushed myself off the couch that I had become cemented into and performed a variation of stretches and jumping jacks to get the blood flowing. To stretch my fingers, I placed my right index and middle fingers on my left palm and pushed them as far back as possible without breaking.

It was sometime around 7:00 p.m. when I finally plugged into the recording console, eight hours after we arrived. I had already heard the same four songs repeated over and over, for hours upon hours, and was becoming delirious.

"Are you ready?" the engineer asked as he swiveled in his chair.

"Let's do this."

Eleven hours after I stepped through the front door of the studio I finished recording the bass parts. I was exhausted and ready to go back to the hotel and pass out. I did a quick search of the studio and realized the rest of the band was gone, and after texting everyone I received a text from Mark.

Be there in ten minutes.

Twenty-minutes later the van arrived at the studio and I climbed into the middle bench seat. I sensed we were not going to the hotel room.

"What were you guys doing?"

"At the fucking Strip club," said Mark.

"Seriously?"

"Yes. And we're going back," he said, raising his hand to show me an ink stamp.

"No."

"I'll pay your cover and buy your first drink."

"Hell fucking no!"

I objected a few more times and then finally surrendered. I knew my pleas were falling on deaf ears.

I remember the club had the stereotypical strip club appearance: Las Vegas style carpet, plush rolling chairs, and a center stage with a shiny, polished pole extending to the ceiling. I remember an obnoxious strip club DJ. I remember watching a girl dance on a stage and buying said girl a shot of tequila then watching her walk away without saying a word. I don't remember leaving the strip club, the drive back to the hotel, the elevator ride, or passing out lengthwise on the bed.

The next morning I got up, showered, and prepared myself for the second day of recording. We arrived at the Blasting Room sometime around 11:00 a.m., and my day consisted of naps on various couches, listening to the guitar and vocal tracks, giving critiques, and attempting to rid myself of the hangover. We finished the final vocal overdubs sometime around 8:00 p.m., having spent nearly twenty-hours recording drums, bass, lead and rhythm guitars, lead vocals, and backing vocals for the four songs. Then they were sent off to be mixed and mastered.

About a month later I had the finished CD in my hands. I slipped it into the CD player of my 1999 Honda Accord and turned the volume up as loud as possible. I didn't care if I blew out my speakers. During the first spin through I listened as a musician, critiquing everything that could have been enhanced, altered, or changed. That wasn't enjoyable. I restarted the CD and listened to the songs as a music lover. From this perspective it sounded good, really good. It was easily the best-sounding collection of songs I had ever recorded. I was proud of the band, what we accomplished, and I was also proud of myself. I had rarely appreciated my musical accomplishments, but this was a moment I relished. I drummed on the steering wheel while I listened to the CD, on repeat over and over and over again.

I felt the album sounded as good as those from bands I considered peers, so I searched the internet for suitable record companies and wrote down every email address and physical address I could find. Most record companies clearly state they don't accept unsolicited material, and all emails and CDs they received would be discarded without being opened. They only accepted music from referrals, and that required a professional manager or agent—we didn't have either. We needed representation for a record company to even open our CD, but most professional agents or managers won't represent bands until they have a high-enough profile. I ignored the warnings and mailed the CDs anyway. The responses were few and far between, but occasionally I received an email from a record company saying thanks, but we're not what they are looking for and wished us good luck.

Our CD release show was on October 3 at the Toad Tavern, two days after my thirty-third birthday. I reckoned that scheduling the show on the same night of my birthday party would maximize the number of people through the door. I was right, the venue was almost at capacity by 9:00 p.m., with about 300 people.

I snuck out of the Toad a few hours before our set to avoid falling into a drunken stupor from the endless offerings of a birthday drink. Sometimes it's easier to disappear than say no to a free drink. I located a secluded location on the side of the laundromat and began returning text messages.

"Scott?" a female voice yelled across the parking lot.

I looked up from my illuminated phone and squinted to decipher the rapidly approaching girl. She continued running, and I was still unsure who it was until she was about ten feet away from me. The girl was Leslie, a friend of a friend of a friend. I'm not exactly sure how we met, but if I had to guess I'd say I met her at one of our shows.

"Happy birthday, Scotty!" she said as she hugged me with such velocity that both of us almost fell onto the sidewalk. After we gathered our balance I noticed two people awkwardly standing off in the distance.

"These are my good friends Josh and Ana," Leslie said.

"Hey guys! Nice to meet you. I'm Scott."

"Hi," Ana said with a contagious smile.

We chatted for a few minutes and sometime during the conversation I glanced up at Ana. She was just standing there with a hand against the brick wall, not doing anything in particular except stealing my heart.

Let's Get It On

(Or Chapter 11)

October 2009 – February 2010

On a first date I would always ask the same question at some point in the conversation: *"Who's your favorite band?"* The question was a test, and if the answer was something like *"I don't have one"* or *"I don't know, I just like whatever's on the radio,"* I knew the date wouldn't go beyond that night. The truth is, I could never date a girl who didn't have a passion for music. To me, it's equivalent to saying you don't have a favorite food and will eat whatever's put on a plate in front of you. I would rather her lie and tell me any band than not be able to name anyone at all. Name a band, any band, fuck I didn't even care if it was Taylor Swift or Britney Spears—at least that's something. I never understood people who don't have a passion for music.

I knew this mentality contributed to my dismal relationship status. I was single and had become a serial dater, going out with a new girl every few months. Over a five-year period, the longest relationship I'd been in was five months. I would end relationships for trivial reasons such as music preferences, clothing style, footwear selection, hairstyle, or because they thought Adam Sandler movies were funny. I even stopped dating a girl once because she forgot to flush the toilet after taking a shit. To say I was a relationship nightmare would be an understatement.

"Get him a fucking body bag, Johnny!" shouted a guy wearing a Heath Ledger-era Joker costume.

"No mercy!" I responded.

"Finish him!"

It was Halloween, and I was dressed as Johnny Lawrence from The Karate Kid. I donned a black karate uniform I purchased from Goodwill and printed iron-on transfers of the Cobra Kai dojo logo, a name tag that said "Johnny," and various patches, including a US flag and yin and yang symbol. A black headband completed the outfit.

We were playing our second annual Halloween show at a venue called Moe's BBQ in Englewood, Colorado. Moe's is a southern-style BBQ restaurant that doubled as a music venue with a capacity of about 250 people. After the dinner rush, usually around nine, they removed the tables and chairs and rolled in a portable soundboard. There's something special about standing on stage with the smell of beef brisket and fried catfish in the air.

Playing on celebratory nights like Halloween, New Year's Eve, St. Patrick's Day, Thanksgiving Eve, and Cinco De Mayo meant there would be a rowdy crowd and an excess of alcohol consumption. Our fans liked to drink to excess almost as much as the band did. The CD release party at the Toad Tavern had set the venue record for highest bar sales in a night, an accomplishment I was unsure how to feel about. The massive consumption of alcohol did include the customary negative consequences like a drunken argument or the occasional fight, mostly by the crowd, and occasionally by the band. I can't say I didn't find those situations somewhat entertaining.

Our set began a little after 11:00 p.m. to a near sold-out crowd of zombies, vampires, ghosts, ghouls, mummies, pirates, Wayne and Garth, Batman, Superman, Spider-Man, Peter and Lois Griffin, a couple flashers, '80s glam bands, metal and hair bands, white trash and trailer trash, and the obligatory sexy nurses, sexy witches, sexy angels, and any other costume an attractive female girl was able to transform into something sexy.

The stage was small, roughly around ten feet wide—about the size of two queen mattresses side by side— and barely fit the four of us and our equipment. It provided very little freedom of movement, and it took skill not to hit Mark or Justin on the back of the head with the headstock of my guitar. The dance floor wasn't much larger, with a capacity of about a hundred people before it bottlenecked into a hallway-type path. The crowd was jammed into the dance floor and against the stage, and someone in the front row could easily spit on our faces if they wanted.

About twenty-minutes into our set I noticed Amy. She'd squeezed through the crowd and position herself against a side wall. She had texted me earlier that day and asked if she could come, and I responded with an unenthusiastic "sure." It's not that I didn't want her to come, I just didn't care if she did. It had been seven years since I walked into her house and saw her clothes scattered on the hallway floor. The hatred slowly faded, until one day it was gone, and I was over it, and over her. I no longer resented her. I just chalked it up to being young.

I also knew she would bring a few friends, and I wanted as many people through the front door as possible. The bigger the audience, the more money we were paid, and the more likelihood that we would get invited to play larger and higher-profile shows. I would invite someone I hated to a show as long as they brought a few paying friends with them.

One of our two covers was a song called "Hello Tomorrow" by a California hybrid rap-rock band called Zebrahead. When Amy and I were dating they were one of our favorite bands and "Hello Tomorrow" was one of her favorite songs. It was a strange coincidence that we were playing that song on the first night Amy decided to see us play.

Mark started the song, and before the intro ended Amy had navigated through the crowd to the side of the stage. During the first verse she drunkenly climbed over a railing and onto the stage, then grabbed the microphone in front of me. She started clearing her throat. I attempted to get her attention, but she was oblivious to me.

Mark looked at me with a "*What the fuck is she doing?*" facial expression. I shrugged. She finally looked at me with a smile then began a side-to-side jig. Imagine a less graceful, completely intoxicated, geriatric version of Axel Rose with a bad hip.

"Do you remember the lyrics?" I whispered into her ear prior to the first chorus.

She nodded in a head-banging fashion. I lacked her confidence.

When the chorus began she forgot the lyrics, ad-libbing parts she couldn't remember and singing out of tune. At one point in the song, someone started throwing ice at her and I almost got hit with friendly fire.

"Give it up for Amy, she did amazing," I said into the microphone at the conclusion of the song. I was instantly met with several boos.

"Get the fuck off the stage you drunk slut!" someone yelled.

We redeemed ourselves by playing the last seven songs close to perfection. The crowd was glued to the stage as the floor bounced to the rhythms of the songs. As the guitars faded, the crowd erupted into thunderous applause. I assumed everyone had forgotten about the mishap with Amy.

Thirty-minutes later I was breaking down my gear when I heard an altercation coming from the front entrance. The stage was roughly 200 feet from the front door, so it was difficult to see exactly what was happening. I jumped off the stage and jogged in an attempt to get a better view, but the crowd swarmed, making it impossible to see any action. I turned around and returned to the stage to resume packing my gear while finishing a warm, flat Bud Light.

After loading out I returned to a sparse crowd, with police officers obtaining statements and six police cars with lights flashing parked on the street directly in front of Moe's. I spotted a friend sitting alone at the bar and sat next to him.

"What the fuck happened?" I said as I removed the sweat-drenched headband.

"Dude, it was fucking crazy. Two girls got jumped by two other girls and they were swinging and throwing punches and pulling hair. I've never seen anything like it before."

"Fuck, I'm sad I missed it. Do you know who it was?"

"I don't. There were fists and screaming and a lot of people trying to break it up."

"Fucking crazy."

"It was!"

"It's pretty awesome a brawl broke out at our show and caused half the Englewood Police Department to show up," I said as I motioned to the bartender.

I ordered a Bud Light and sat at the bar watching police cars drive away one by one.

I awoke the next morning with a text from Amy.

Please call me ASAP!

I flung my sheets off and sat at the end of the bed with my hands in my face. My head was pounding. I called Amy back, and she instantly went into a tirade about getting sucker-punched by my friend Jackie. She said her nose might be broken, she was going to have a pile of medical bills, and she wanted to press assault charges. She talked for a few minutes straight before I got a word in.

"I need you to be my witness and tell the cops what happened."

"Witness to what?"

"Me getting jumped!"

"I didn't see it so I can't be a witness."

"I just told you what happened."

"But that's your side of the story."

There was a long silence and I could feel her frustration through the phone.

"Are you going to take her side?"

"I'm not taking either side. I just didn't see what happened."

"But I told you! She fucking attacked me. She jumped me from behind and probably broke my nose."

"That's what I heard from you."

"We've known each other forever—and you think I'm lying?"

"I don't think you're lying, but I can't say that's what happened because I didn't see it."

There was another silence. She coughed and cleared her throat.

"What are you going to say when the detective calls you?" she asked.

"That I was on stage, packing up my gear and I didn't see who started the fight. I imagine it's going to be a short conversation."

"Fuck you, Scott!" Amy said as she hung up.

I dropped the phone into my lap and stared out my bedroom window for a few moments. I wanted to help her, I really did, but I wasn't about to lie for Amy even though I had a strong suspicion Jackie sucker-punched her. I chalked it up as karma for Amy cheating on me almost a decade earlier.

I was standing on the stage of the Marquis Theater and looking down at our seven-song set list taped to the monitor speaker. The Marquis was a medium-sized venue with a capacity of about 400 people, located in downtown Denver a couple blocks from Coors Field, home of the Colorado Rockies. The room was lively, with PA music blasting and drinks being served to the sold-out crowd.

We were opening for a California punk band called Guttermouth. The band was infamous for being banned from Canada for eighteen months due to public indecency charges, as well as getting kicked off the 2004 Warped Tour for mocking other bands while onstage. They never reached mainstream success like other California punk bands, such as Green Day and the Offspring, but they were legends within the punk scene. They could tour the country and sell a few hundred tickets every night, and they had been doing so for over two decades by the time we opened for them.

I grabbed my phone off my speaker and pressed the on button to illuminate the screen. The time displayed 8:56—four minutes before our set time. I inspected my guitar, looking up and down the neck from bridge to headstock. It was beaten up. The front strap post had snapped off and the strap was held in place with about half a roll of duct tape, one of the tuning pegs was bent, chunks of paint were chipped away from the orange body, a volume knob was missing and there was dirt and sweat strewn all over the body and neck. Punk rock isn't meant to be perfect, and my bass exhibited that.

The lights were blinding, and I squinted out into the crowd searching for recognizable faces among the sea of strangers. I saw Ana across the floor at the bar and she began to wave. I was about to wave back when the lights dimmed and the house music faded. The crowd let out a thunderous cheer as Mark approached the microphone.

Travis hit his sticks together and the music began. By the bridge of the first song Mark had what looked like half the crowd clapping to the beat of Travis's bass drum.

"Let me see your hands!" Mark yelled into the microphone.

Mark had charisma and was a great front man, which isn't an easy thing. He could sing and entertain while having organic interactions with the crowd. When it comes to being a solid front man, you either are or you aren't. Over the years I had seen countless talented singers who didn't have good stage presence—they were awkward and it was sometimes uncomfortable to watch. But to Mark, engaging with the crowd was second nature, and they hung on his every word.

Forty-five minutes later, I was standing in the lobby behind a folding table that had our merchandise neatly displayed on its white, plastic surface. There was a piece of paper taped to the table listing the prices for our merchandise.

CDs - $5
Shirts - $8
CD/Shirt Combo - $10
Stickers - FREE!

I almost always made a deal—especially after a couple drinks—with anyone who showed interest, usually offering them at or around cost. I probably gave away as many CDs and T-Shirts as we sold. Truth be told, I considered it a win if we broke even after a show. I preferred getting merchandise into the hands of a fan over making a few dollars in profit.

I was about to close a T-shirt transaction when I heard an altercation across the lobby between a guy and, I assumed, his girlfriend. The guy was very drunk and had the appearance of someone who was just released from jail. He was pissed about something she did, and the yelling quickly escalated into a shoving match between the two. He gave the impression that he was moments from punching her.

"I'll be right back," I said to the potential customer.

I rushed over and attempted to intervene.

"How about you go outside to calm down?"

"Who the fuck are you?" he scowled as he clenched his fist turning it towards me.

"Just go outside and get some fresh air," I said, raising my hands in a non-confrontational manner.

He stared blankly at me.

Guttermouth was playing and it was loud, very loud, but I could hear him panting. My hands were shaking, and I mentally prepared myself for my first fight in over a decade. The ordeal had only been twenty seconds or so, but it felt like I was standing there for minutes.

I took my focus off him and looked around the lobby. A crowd of people had formed a circle around the three of us. I was waiting for security guards or anyone else to intervene and dissuade him from starting a fight. I waited, but no such luck.

He lunged and tackled me, Lawrence Taylor–style, knocking over a high-top table and chair in the process. I collapsed to the ground and made my best attempt to avoid hitting my head on the tile and getting a concussion.

I was momentarily disoriented, and when I realized what happened he was hovering over me with a daunting look on his face. I closed my eyes and prepared myself for either a punch to the face or a kick to the stomach. I didn't get either. He turned around and ran out the front door.

I don't know if it was the adrenaline or because I wanted to redeem myself, but I jumped to my feet and chased him out of the Marquis then north on Larimer Street, sprinting through crowds of drunk people and past parking meters, trashcans, newspaper stands, and light poles wrapped with show flyers.

I continued the chase for two city blocks into a parking lot when the adrenaline rush ceased and I realized I didn't have a plan of action if I caught up to him. I didn't want to have to fight the guy alone, and by his appearance he was accustomed to back-alley fights and didn't care if they resulted in a jail visit. I, on the other hand didn't want to spend the night in jail with a pending assault charge.

The sprint rapidly declined until I was completely stopped. I watched him zigzag between vehicles until he vanished into a dark parking lot with a view of the downtown Denver skyline in the distance. I turned around and slowly walked back to the Marquis.

When I returned there was a group of people congregating on the sidewalk in front of the Marquis. Ana looked up and saw me returning then beelined straight towards me.

"That was freaking amazing," she said as she kissed me on the cheek.

I was taken aback by the kiss—and confused by it. I briefly thought she was interested in me but concluded that was a crazy notion. I was reading too much into the gesture I told myself. She was happily married, and it was nothing more than a drunken friendly kiss on the cheek.

"I want to sleep with you," Ana said.

It was a few weeks after the Guttermouth show and we were having happy hour margaritas at Chili's. I knew what she said, but I couldn't comprehend it. I had always been naïve at times and often missed obvious signals from girls. I sometimes didn't know someone was romantically interested until we were making out. Apparently that kiss on the cheek was one of those signals I misinterpreted.

After the CD release show in October Ana and I casually started emailing, and that transitioned into instant messaging, which led to exchanging numbers, which turned into texting daily. After about two months I was talking to Ana more than anyone else in my life. On most days she was the first person I texted after waking up and the last person I texted before going to bed. I knew it wasn't normal for a single guy to continuously be texting with a married woman, but I figured if she was fine with the situation I was as well. I assumed we were good friends, and nothing more. I assumed Ana felt the same about me.

We talked about everything. I told her stories about bachelor life and she told me stories about married life. She trusted me and confided in me about her marriage. She told me she and Josh fought constantly, that she felt like they were closer to roommates than husband and wife, and that they hadn't slept together in almost six months. She suspected Josh was cheating on her.

After her proposal my stomach dropped, and I became tense, anxious, and scared all at once. I nervously stared at the colorful Southwestern-themed table top then looked past Ana to the basketball highlights playing behind her on SportsCenter. I was searching for something, anything to say, because I sensed she expected my response to be something profound.

I remember saying something clumsy like "Umm—what did you say?"

We were both disappointed with my response.

"I'm sorry, I shouldn't have said anything."

"No, it's fine. I just wasn't expecting you to say that. I'm trying to comprehend it."

"Did I just fuck up our friendship?"

"No! Of course not."

She sipped her margarita and stared out the window, taking in the vast shopping center parking lot.

"I haven't been happy in a long time, and I'm just really fucking confused," she said. "I probably should have just kept my mouth shut, but I had to tell you how I feel. You've become one of my closest friends and I don't want to jeopardize that."

"You're one of my closest friends too and there is nothing you can say or do to change that. I promise."

She paused and raised her glass, "Cheers to awkward situations."

"Cheers."

We talked for another hour without mentioning the proposal, but it was the only thing I could think about. I didn't start talking with Ana because I wanted to sleep with her, or because I was interested in her romantically, or any other scandalous reason. But I also couldn't lie and say I hadn't thought about it.

She was accurate that sleeping together would jeopardize our friendship, in fact, I almost certainly knew that would end it. A friend of mine had slept with a married woman, and after the sexual encounter she felt guilty and mended her marriage. She emailed my friend saying it was an enormous mistake and to never contact her again. I had a feeling I was destined for the same email.

I was in a moral and sexual dilemma. My brain and penis were caught in a chess match. I had never slept with a married woman, and I would be venturing into new territory. I didn't want to be the catalyst of a divorce or get my ass kicked by an angry husband. But I also felt special for being asked, in a depraved, adulterous, immoral sort of way. I wasn't proud of myself for considering it, but if she was determined to have an affair, I'd rather it be with me than someone else.

We paid the bill and I walked her to her car. We hugged and said goodbye. In the process of closing her door, she stopped and looked up at me.

"The offer is still on the table so think about it and let me know," she said, then shut the door.

I went home and sat in silence with my phone in my lap. I wasn't sure how to proceed and decided a beer should assist me in the decision-making process. That beer turned into two, then that quickly doubled to four, then I lost count.

I grabbed my phone and feverishly typed into the keypad.

Let's do it.

I slowly exhaled then sent the message. I threw the phone to the opposite side of the couch. I stared at the back of the phone then looked away to the reflection of the blank TV screen. A few minutes later the phone started to vibrate against the cushion. I stretched out until I reached the phone, then rolled over and positioned it on my chest. I remained motionless in the dark and quiet room for a long time, until I got up the courage to view the text message.

Great! We will figure out the details soon. :)

I chuckled, amused she concluded the adultery plan text with a smiley face.

A little after ten on a Thursday night, I glanced at the five empty Bud Light cans on my kitchen table. I was halfway through the sixth. I was drinking to settle my nerves, but it wasn't helping in the least. I considered taking multiple shots of whiskey as well, but I didn't want to be too drunk for our encounter and not be able to get an erection.

She told her husband she was meeting friends for dinner and drinks and would be home around 11:30 p.m., then when she met up with her friends, she told them that she only could stay out until 9:30 p.m. because she had to be at work early the following morning. That was her master plan, and it seemed flimsy to me. It was a thirty-minute drive from the bar to my apartment and another twenty-minute drive from my apartment to Ana's, so we would approximately have one hour and ten minutes to commence and complete the affair.

I had never been in a situation where the first sexual encounter was planned out in advance, and I wasn't sure of the exact etiquette. Was I supposed to offer her a glass of wine and follow that with conversation until the moment felt right, or was I supposed to rip off her clothes the moment she walked into the apartment and bend her over the couch? It was all new to me, and it was nerve-racking. I knew Ana must have felt tenfold because the consequences for her were far greater, she had a marriage, family, and friends to lose. My worst-case scenario was getting into a fight with her husband.

Sometime around 9:35 p.m. there was a knock on the door. I jumped off the couch and tiptoed towards it. I stealthily placed my hands onto the door, leaned in, closed my right eye, and peered through the peep hole.

It was Ana. She was wearing a puffy winter parka with a feather-lined hood that was pulled down and practically covered half her face. She was bobbing her head side to side and it looked like she was singing the chorus of a song. To my surprise, she gave off the impression that she was excited.

"Please, please—please don't let me fuck this up," I whispered to myself.

I took a deep breath, licked my lips, and placed my hand on the door knob. I turned the knob and pulled back, and as the door opened she pulled back the hood and smiled. She stood there under the porch light and stared at me with her emerald-green eyes. They were mesmerizing. I knew there was no turning back.

"Scott!" she yelled as she ran in for a hug.

She jumped onto my body, wrapped her arms around me, and buried her head into my chest. We hugged in the hallway for a few minutes. I attempted to break it off early twice, but she was not having it, each time she tightened her grip. After the hug concluded she sat on the couch and I went into the kitchen to prepare drinks. I assumed she needed one, I knew I did.

"Do you want a beer or whiskey or a vodka drink or something?"

"I just did two shots before I left so I'm pretty buzzed. I probably don't need a drink, but I'll sip on a beer if you have one."

"I can do that."

I removed two Bud Lights from the refrigerator, wiped the sweat off my palms with a hand towel then returned to the living room. Ana had removed her coat and shoes and was sitting cross-legged on one side of the couch. I didn't want to sit too close to her, so I decided an arm's length away was an appropriate, comfortable distance.

"Here you go," I said as I handed her a beer.

"Thanks."

"How was the bar?"

"It was fun."

"Cool."

I leaned back and took a drink. Then Ana took a drink. Then we sat in silence, which evolved into an even longer silence. We looked at each other, smiled, and then looked away.

"So . . ." she finally said breaking the silence.

"Yes?"

"How are we supposed to do this?"

"I figured you would know."

"How would I know? I've never done this before and I definitely never pictured myself with anyone other than Josh."

She was blinking erratically, and she looked like she was about to collapse into her lap and start crying. I placed my hand on her knee in an attempt to ease the situation.

"We don't have to do this, I promise. We can just sit here and talk," I said.

"Thank you."

Twenty-minutes later she was topless and unbuttoning her pants while I was opening a condom wrapper.

Nevermind

(Or Chapter 12)

March 2010 – July 2010

Before Ana left my apartment that night, we constructed our infidelity plan.

"I think we should avoid talking or texting for two weeks. It'll be easier if we avoid each other entirely for a while," I said.

"Agreed. This also has to be a one-time thing. Maybe after I figure everything out we can try it again."

"Deal," I said, as we shook hands.

The following morning I awoke to my cell phone vibrating on my nightstand.

I don't think I can go 2 days without talking to you, let alone 2 weeks!!

We slept together again three days later and made another infidelity plan, then slept together again four days after that. We continued sleeping together and continued to pledge not to do it again. We finally gave up on the pledge after the fourth unsuccessful attempt. I knew the longer the situation continued, the harder it would be to stop and the more disastrously it would end.

February turned into March, then May, and the "one-time fling" turned into a multiple month-long affair. We were hanging out two to three times a week, and most of our close friends had become aware of our secret relationship.

I admit it, I was morally flawed. I had been cheated on, and knew what it felt like, and I should have never done it. I knew better, but I was selfish. Ana made me happy, and I ignored the heartbreak it would cause her family to satisfy my own desires. I didn't go out searching for someone who was married, and she didn't get married with the intention of cheating on her husband. It just happened. We met and fell in love, and unfortunately for both of us, she was married.

On the first Saturday in May, we were having drinks at a bar on the 16th Street Mall in downtown Denver when Ana saw a couple who were old neighbors. She quickly began fabricating a story and filling me in on the details.

"We randomly ran into each other and decided to grab a drink to catch up," she said. She was on the verge of a panic attack.

"Calm down, we'll be fine. We're just two friends having a drink, nothing more."

I was ready. I had been preparing myself for this type of predicament and knew I'd probably have to talk myself out of a complicated situation at some point. I considered fabricating a lie to old acquaintances to be a difficulty level of three. Family members would increase the difficulty to six or seven, and her husband—with any combination of his friends—would be a ten. I wasn't sure if I could talk my way out of that situation.

It turned out to be a false alarm and the couple just resembled her neighbors, but I knew we were pushing our luck, and that luck would eventually run out. Denver has a small-town feel where it seems like everyone knows each other, and I knew sooner or later we would actually run into someone that knew her or her husband.

It was tiring, and I only had to prepare myself for situations that involved her acquaintances. I couldn't imagine how stressful it must have been for her, she was practically living a double life. Family and marriage by day, affair by night. I knew if we continued there would be a breaking point when the weight of the affair would fall back onto itself, like a collapsing star. As much as I wanted to continue, I knew we had to end it before there were disastrous consequences.

I selected the second Saturday in May as the time to end the relationship. I was leaving on a small Midwest tour the following weekend, and Ana was going to Hawaii for a wedding during the first week of June. We were both going to be out of town and away from each other, so it felt like the ideal time.

We were sitting in an oversized booth in a family-owned Mexican restaurant near my apartment. We went there about once a week. I didn't select the place for the quality of the food, I selected it for the seclusion. It was usually empty, and I knew the odds of bumping into someone we knew were virtually zero.

"We have to end this until you're separated," I said.

"Tonight?"

I nodded. Ana stared at me, expressionless, then looked down at the plate of enchiladas and watered-down margarita. She was about to respond, but stopped just as the first word was about to escape her lips.

"You know I'm right," I said.

"Okay," she said with her eyes closed.

After dinner, we went to a park and then walked onto the baseball field within its confines. We lay on the center field grass for what felt like an hour and watched constellations twinkle through a cloudy sky backdrop. A train whistle thundered in the far distance as Ana breathed heavily on my chest.

"Fuck it, let's just pack up and move to Mexico and start over," Ana said.

"I don't speak Spanish, so that might be tough."

"Yeah, me either."

"This is only temporary. I promise."

"I hope so," she said as she squeezed my hand.

We were booked for a short weekend tour that began on Friday night in Lincoln, Nebraska, and then would transverse east along I-80 until we arrived in Des Moines the following night. The schedule was tight: leave Friday morning around 7:00 a.m., arrive in Lincoln sometime Friday afternoon, play Friday night, leave Lincoln sometime in the middle of the night, drive the last three hours to Des Moines, sleep Saturday morning, play Saturday night, then either crash on a couch or sleep in the van, wake up Sunday morning, drive the nine hours back to Denver, and arrive back in Denver by Sunday night to sleep then wake up Monday morning just in time to return to work. On paper, the itinerary looked a lot less complicated.

Nebraska/Iowa Tour:
Denver to Lincoln: 7 hours /488 miles
Lincoln to Des Moines: 3 hours/186 miles
Des Moines to Denver: 9 hours/674 miles
Total Trip: 19 hours/1348 miles

My preferred weekend tour locations were major cities like Salt Lake City, Las Vegas, Phoenix, and Albuquerque, but occasionally we opted for less glamorous musical destinations of Nebraska and Iowa. We booked a Midwest tour because Justin, our second guitar player, grew up in a small town a few hours south of Des Moines and he lived there in his early 20s before moving to Denver. He had connections with booking managers at different venues in Des Moines and had friends and family within the city limits. That guaranteed we would be playing in front of more than just the bar staff.

Geographically speaking, Denver is not the ideal location for a band that wants to tour. The town is somewhat isolated from other major cities, which means more drive time and gas money go into any tour. The nearest metropolis is Salt Lake City, at a little under eight hours. A band in southern California, on the other hand, could start a tour in San Diego and pass through Los Angeles, San Francisco, and Sacramento in a little over nine hours, and a band on the East Coast could drive from Boston to New York to Philadelphia to Baltimore to Washington D.C. in almost the same time it takes to drive from Denver to Salt Lake City. Bands on either coast can play larger cities with less drive time and lower travel expenses. It was a real disadvantage for a band living in Denver, but I guess that's the trade-off for living in an amazing city.

The vehicle for the trip was a black Chevy van nicknamed "Black Betty" and had close to 200,000 miles on the odometer. We used Black Betty for shows around the Denver metro area, but this was the first time we were taking her on tour. I was always concerned about driving a twenty-year-old van with a few hundred thousand miles across state lines, but we didn't have the luxury of a tour bus or the finances for a van that was manufactured sometime in the 2000s.

We arrived in Lincoln a little after 5:00 p.m., parked in front of Knickerbockers, unloaded our gear, then walked to the closest bar to commence the weekend of music and drinking in the Cornhusker and Hawkeye states.

The show started around 8 p.m. and was completely uneventful. Two subpar local bands opened, and then we played in front of about fifty people who were scattered throughout the venue. We were paid $125 for our performance, and sold about fifty dollars' worth of merchandise, or the equivalent of one tank of gas for Black Betty.

"What the fuck are we going to do now?" Mark asked as we loaded the last guitar case into the van and shut the back doors.

There were three possible options:

1. Get a hotel room.
2. Leave Lincoln and drive the three hours to Des Moines.
3. Stay in Lincoln and continue drinking until last call and pass out in the van.

I didn't want to get a room for two reasons. The first was that it cost money, and that money would come out of the band account that barely had enough money to cover the gas for the trip. The second was that I wasn't concerned about a bed or sleep. I was fortunate that I could get a decent sleep on almost any surface and in any position. I had no qualms about sleeping in the passenger seat of Black Betty, and I'd virtually get the same level of sleep there as I would in a bed.

I also voted against driving to Des Moines. I didn't want to spend the next three hours in a van driving on a dark, unfamiliar interstate. It would also give us an arrival time of four or five in the morning. I had never been to Des Moines, but I imagined the nightlife at that time was close to nothing.

"I say we stay here and get drunk," I said.

"That works for me," Travis responded.

"Me too," said Justin.

We were discussing our plan on the O Street sidewalk, about a mile north of the Nebraska State Capitol and a mile south of the main campus of the University of Nebraska, when two guys who were at our show approached us and began a conversation.

"Are you guys staying in town?" one of the guys asked.

"I think so," Mark said.

"Oh shit! Want us to show you guys around?" the other guy asked.

We all looked at each other, and then nodded in unison.

"Sure, why not," I said.

We walked O Street, stopping in what felt like every third bar for beers, shots, and sometimes shots inside of a beer. One bar offered fishbowls filled with mixed drinks that were forty-eight ounces, the equivalent of four drinks. Travis drank his in under ten minutes, instantly putting him to the front of the line in our race to inebriation.

As we continued east on O Street, the vibrant nightlife quickly dissipated into office buildings and empty parking lots. The people disappeared, and the music faded.

"This is the end of the line guys. You can try that strip club but I don't recommend it," one of the locals said.

I stared at the crudely painted black door of a strip club named "The Foxy Lady." The place looked run-down, and closer to a crack house than an upscale strip club. I imagined girls who got naked there were either pushing fifty or weighing as much as an offensive lineman. The prospects of seeing high-level talent didn't seem promising.

I thought about walking back to Black Betty and calling Ana. It was after midnight, but Lincoln is on Central Standard Time so it was only eleven in Denver. I imagined she would be up and probably wanted to talk to me as much as I wanted to talk to her. We hadn't seen each other since our proclaimed final night and had only sent the occasional text since.

I was second-guessing the decision to stop talking to her, and wondering if I had made a mistake. I missed her, but I also didn't miss the stress of dating a married woman, the careful planning of every meeting, the lies and deceit, the sneaking around, the preparation of ironclad alibis, and the fear of getting jumped. I knew ending the affair was the honorable decision, but my heart didn't give a fuck about being honorable. It didn't feel right, but sometimes tough choices never do.

"Are you fucking coming?" Mark yelled to me, his hand on the door handle of the Foxy Lady.

"Yeah, I'm coming."

The interior was exactly how I envisioned: small, dark, and dirty. The paint was fading and decrepit and the color scheme appeared to be from the 1980s. The tables and chairs were worn, unmatched, and stain-covered, and the room had an awful stench that was a combination of cigarette smoke, stale beer, and cheap sex. I felt like I'd catch an STD by touching anything within the establishment, so I proceeded with caution.

One stage in the center of the room had exposed pipes above it, and dancers would grab onto and swing from them during their performances. There were no DJs and not even a jukebox, which I had seen in less classy strip clubs, the source of music at the Foxy Lady was a Sony portable CD Boombox that probably cost about forty dollars at Wal-Mart. The dancer would select a disc from a book of CDs, put the disc in the stereo, press Play, and start dancing. During one performance "Closer" by Nine Inch Nails started skipping, and the dancer had to remove her legs from the shoulders of a patron, walk to the stereo, and skip to the next song.

I was wrong about the talent, though. Most of the dancers were surprisingly attractive. I surmised since we were mere blocks from the University of Nebraska campus some of the girls were dancing to help pay for tuition.

I was sipping on a vodka and soda when I glanced up and saw a Katy Perry doppelgänger preparing to perform. I wondered if looking like Katy Perry provided a benefit to her stripping career or a point of shame because she resembled one of the most famous pop stars in the world and was showing her vagina for singles.

I sat down at her stage, removed three singles from my pocket and positioned them on the dance platform in front of me. She danced for the entirety of the first song without approaching anyone. She kept her eyes closed and gave off the appearance that she was dancing alone, not in front of sleazy guys waiting patiently for her to remove her clothes.

I strangely felt something of a connection with her. On countless occasions I felt uninterested while performing to an unresponsive audience, and to escape I would close my eyes and envision that I was playing at Red Rocks to a sold-out crowd of thousands. I was hoping she was doing the same—envisioning that she was dancing on Broadway or performing for Cirque du Soleil. That made me feel much better about my intention to hand her money in exchange for seeing her topless.

At the start of the second song she circled the entire stage and pushed every dollar bill into the center. She removed her top and approached every guy that was watching her dance, giving them her complete attention. When it was finally my turn she played with my hair and squeezed her cleavage into my face.

"Thank you, sweetie," she whispered as she bit the top of my earlobe.

The third and final song came and went and so did twenty dollars. I spent my allotted stripper budget on one girl in under fifteen minutes. I ordered another vodka drink and retreated to a back table to watch from a distance, and avoid blowing my entire tour budget on an unplanned strip club visit.

An hour later we exited the Foxy Lady and I stumbled the half-mile back to the van. I had the feeling that I was going to throw up and knew if I stayed awake it would definitely happen, so I passed out within minutes of returning to Black Betty. We departed Lincoln that night and drove straight to Des Moines, arriving sometime in the early dawn hours.

The next day consisted of sleeping, drinking, exploring downtown Des Moines, dropping quarters into a Big Buck

Hunter arcade game, and even a trip to the batting cages. I attempted the 75 mph cage and only connected with three out of twelve baseballs. Essentially, we were doing anything that was relatively cheap in order to kill time until soundcheck that night.

The Des Moines show was at a venue called Vaudeville Mews and was virtually identical to the Lincoln show: same crowd size and same payout, but we sold less merchandise. The revenue from both shows totaled $325, or probably the equivalent of what the four of us spent on alcohol during the trip.

After the show we went to a house party in West Des Moines and continued drinking. The hosts were friends of Justin, and they started a bonfire that reached about twenty feet high. It was quite the spectacle and something I'd never seen in Denver, or anywhere else. I watched the embers float through the black sky and started to lose my balance. I reached out and grabbed the back of a plastic lawn chair, which helped stabilize my stance. I decided the near-mishap was my cue to call it a night.

"I'm going to bed," I yelled to whoever was listening.

I walked to the van, opened the side door, and crawled onto the floorboard. I rested my head onto a makeshift pillow that I made from a hoodie. I looked at my phone and the time displayed 4:34. We had to be on the highway by nine or ten at the latest to arrive in Denver before midnight. Mark, Travis, and Justin were still drinking around the bonfire and I had a strong feeling our departure time would be in jeopardy. I set my alarm for 9:00 a.m. and closed my eyes.

Buzz, buzz, buzz.

I awoke to the vibration of my phone against my cheek. I was still on the floor of the van, and I could feel the sunlight penetrating through the gigantic windows of Black Betty. My head was throbbing, and my mouth was parched with the remnants of rancid Bud Light on my breath. I slowly began to open my eyes, but the sunlight was blinding.

"Fuck this," I muttered.

I removed the crusties from my eye crevices and slowly began to open them. I was disoriented, and it took me a few minutes to grasp the situation. My first observation was that the van wasn't moving—and the engine wasn't even running. I pulled myself up to a sitting position and saw Mark in the passenger seat, passed out.

I pushed myself off the dirt-infested carpet and onto the middle bench seat. This minimal movement made me dizzy, and I realized I was still extremely inebriated. The alcohol in my system seemed to intensify with every change in position. I looked outside and noticed numerous cars and red shopping carts, then familiar red lettering with a bullseye sign on the facade of a building.

"What the fuck are we doing in a Target parking lot?" I asked as I shook Mark.

Nothing. He was completely comatose. I picked up my phone, and after my blurry vision finally came into focus the digital numbers displayed 11:18.

I began doing the calculations, using all ten fingers to assist with the math. I had a hunch we were still in the Des Moines city limits, and if that was the case it meant we hadn't even begun the nine-hour drive back home. Add in an hour loss due to the time zone change, and our estimated time of arrival in Denver would be 11:30 p.m.—and that was if we were on the road in the next fifteen minutes.

Travis was passed out on the back bench seat, Justin was on the floor below him, and Mark was still motionless. I knew no one would be capable of driving and made the executive decision that for us to have any chance of making it back to Denver before midnight, I was going to have to drive.

"I need breakfast. Yes, breakfast will definitely help with this fucking drive," I said, attempting to subconsciously trick myself into thinking food would help.

I gathered myself, exited the van, and strolled into the Target. I looked bad and probably smelled worse. I did my best to avoid eye contact with anyone. When I got a whiff of the café, the smell incited a gag reaction and I almost vomited on myself.

I walked directly to the café and grabbed two slices of pizza, a pretzel, and a thirty-two ounce lemon-lime Gatorade. I was hoping the carbohydrate load would absorb the alcohol in my stomach and assist in the sobering-up process. I knew the only real assistance would be time and sleep, but they were luxuries I didn't have.

I devoured the pizza and pretzel in about four minutes. I considered getting more food but decided against it. I didn't want to get sick or have diarrhea from a combination of booze and overeating. I left the café and walked back to Black Betty.

Upon arrival at the van I started doing jumping jacks, then dropped to the pavement and did ten pushups, then jumped back up to do more jumping jacks. My heart rate was up and my blood was flowing. I was out of breath, delirious, sleep-deprived, and still drunk. It probably wasn't the best time to get behind the wheel of a two-ton vehicle. I opened the driver door then sat in the captain's chair, pulled the seatbelt around my waist, and turned the key. The engine was deafening.

"Alright boys, you ready to go home?" I yelled as I turned around, checking to see if there was any sort of reaction. Nothing.

"Let's fucking go!" I shouted.

I pulled the gear shift into drive, stomped on the throttle, and sped out of the parking lot. After driving in circles for about five minutes I located the highway on-ramp. I was feeling more confident about my driving abilities until I saw a road sign stating the mileage to Kansas City and realized I was driving on I-35 in the wrong direction. I took the next exit, drove across the overpass, and followed the signs displaying I-35 north. Twenty-minutes later I was driving west on I-80, on my way to the Iowa plains, then onto Omaha, Lincoln, and the Nebraska plains. By nightfall we would be in Colorado then the Rocky Mountains and home.

I glanced at the speedometer, which showed that I was driving 62 mph, a couple mph under the speed limit. I knew driving under the speed limit would only extend the drive time, but I set a goal to arrive in Lincoln without getting pulled over or falling asleep. I always considered goals important, even minuscule ones that almost anyone with a driver's license and a heartbeat could accomplish.

"Make it to Lincoln, then make one of these assholes drive, and I'll get to sleep the rest of the way home."

Alcohol toxins were emitting through everyone's pores and the van smelled like a brewery. I could almost taste the alcohol in the air. I rolled down the window to get a breath of fresh air, but it offered little help against the pungent odor.

At some point on I-80 there was a cluster of huge wind turbines that dotted the landscape. It was renewable energy in all its glory. I would guess they were at least one or two hundred feet tall, and the blades appeared to be moving in slow motion. Unconsciously, I started oscillating my head in circular movements in unison with the enormous blades.

Two hours into the drive I was still drunk. I could feel every bump and crack in the highway, and it rattled my head while intensifying my hangover. I had a premonition the hangover wouldn't diminish until we reached the Colorado border. I turned around and saw everyone was still passed out, and then turned back to the endless stretch of highway before me. My eyes began to get heavy as the van slowly drifted closer and closer to the shoulder. I considered pulling over and attempting to make someone else drive, but I knew the results would be fruitless, and I'd probably still windup behind the steering wheel. I also felt somewhat obligated to continue driving since I had gotten the most sleep.

The sounds of the drive were hypnotizing, and I was worried they'd lull me into a slumber. I didn't want to jerk awake with Black Betty traveling at a high speed on the gravel shoulder and have to make a last-ditch effort to stop the van from rolling over countless times in an Iowa corn field. I did everything I could to stay awake, including drinking black coffee, punching myself, rolling down the window, and eating sunflower seeds—I even briefly considered masturbating.

This was the same lonely, desolate highway that killed John Holohan, drummer of the New Jersey rock band Bayside. The band was en route to Salt Lake City, traveling west on I-80 a few miles outside of Cheyenne, Wyoming, when the van hit a patch of black ice, skidded off the road, and flipped over numerous times. Holohan was killed instantly, and other band members and the crew were injured.

"Don't fucking fall asleep," I said as I steered with one hand and punched my calf with the other.

Rumours

(Or Chapter 13)

October 2010 – November 2010

In the summer of 2010, the band entered an independent studio in Denver and came out with a five-song EP. We scheduled the CD release show for October 2 at Summit Music Hall in the LoDo neighborhood of downtown Denver. The Summit was a music venue-turned-dance club-turned-back into-music venue with a capacity of about 900.

The show was a day after my thirty-fourth birthday, and I was fully aware I was one year away from my self-imposed musical expiration date. I wasn't concerned about the expiration date, though, because I was having fun playing and the band was having a banner year. Our audiences continued to grow larger and larger, we were opening for higher-profile national bands on a monthly basis, recorded two EPs, and received a nomination for Best Denver Punk Band by *Westword*, the local alternative weekly newspaper.

As good as the band was going, my personal life was on the opposite end of the spectrum. I was a mess, and my relationship choices were closer to that of a teenager than someone who was nearing middle age. I attempted to date, but those attempts were futile. I still had feelings for Ana, and I compared every new dating prospect was to her—leading all of them to fail miserably.

After I returned from Iowa and she returned from Hawaii, we returned to our lives prior to meeting. I went most of June and all of July without talking to her, but on one morning in early August I looked at my phone and saw a text message.

Hey stranger! Long time no talk. Wondering if you'd like to grab dinner and catch up soon.

I stared at the screen. I wanted to curse her for texting me, but I also wanted to see her. I was unsure if I should delete the message or write back asking when and where. After a few moments I finally began typing.

That would be cool. Let me know what works for you.

I met Ana for dinner a few days later at a sports bar inside a Holiday Inn. We shared a pepperoni pizza and a pitcher of Bud Light, paid the check, and had sex in the backseat of my Accord in a secluded section of the parking lot under a tree. I was worried a guest walking to their car would stumble upon us, but any apprehension vanished twenty seconds after she took off her pants.

We continued seeing each other for a couple weeks after the Holiday Inn rendezvous, but she abruptly vanished and went into radio silence. I didn't hear from her for a few weeks, then we started talking again and the pattern repeated itself. For August and September our relationship was two weeks on, two weeks off. Two weeks of dating then two weeks of nothing. I was frustrated and suspected I was being used. I had never been used before, and I felt guilty for acting similarly to girls in the past.

This on-and-off cycle continued until a few days before my birthday, when the relationship recommenced.

Ana was sitting on my couch, and I was lying on the floor with a 102-degree fever and what felt like the onset of the flu.

"You can go home if you want. I'm zero fun so I completely understand," I said.

"Are you crazy? I'm not going anywhere. You're sick, and I'm going to stay here and take care of you."

I remained motionless on the floor with hot and cold sweats while Ana did her best attempt to comfort me. She forced me to eat chicken soup and drink Gatorade, and ran her fingers through my hair until I passed out.

I awoke the next morning and walked out to the kitchen. I glanced down and there was a neatly folded piece of paper on the table.

I love you so much, so much more than you could ever know. I am sorry I ever did this to us. If the situation was different, it would have never been hard and I know I could have made you happy. You are really the best thing that has happened to me.

I felt like an asshole for doubting her motives, but I perceived this as a goodbye note. I read the note a couple more times before I dropped it and ran into the bathroom, dropping to my knees as vomit erupted out of my mouth, splashing onto the white porcelain.

The CD release show was scheduled to start at 8:00 p.m., and our set time was 10:45 to 12:00. I wasn't sure if I was going to be able to play. I still had a high fever and was paralyzed on a couch backstage. I watched as everyone drank beer and did shots in preparation for the show. My preparation was sipping on Pedialyte and praying I wouldn't pass out on stage.

I wanted the night to be over, and I briefly considered canceling the show, but I knew the rest of the band would've been infuriated if I even suggested it. We also sold close to $1,000 in pre-sale tickets, so it wasn't even a possibility.

I constructed a seemingly simple plan for the night: spend the majority of the evening listening to the bands from the couch backstage, mixed in with the occasional bathroom break, while socializing as little as possible. Once our set began, I'd attempt to play the songs as well as I could, with as much enthusiasm as I could muster, while trying not to faint from exhaustion on stage under the bright, sweltering lights. Then, after our twelve-song set, I'd rush to the merchandise table and attempt to sell as many CDs and T-shirts as possible. Once the venue was empty I'd break down my gear, load it into the van, and finally go home. It would only be a mere six hours until I'd have my head on either my pillow or the bathroom tile.

As the night progressed I started to feel better, and I hadn't vomited in almost eight hours, an achievement I was proud of.

"You really look like shit, are you going to be able to make it?" Mark asked.

I slowly lifted my head with raised eyebrows. "Yeah, I think so," I muttered.

"Good, I was a little worried about you. Let's go out there and fucking rock it!" he said as he patted me on the knee.

As the set time approached the fever virtually disappeared, and by the time I was standing on stage tuning my bass I felt fine. Actually, I felt better than fine—I'd go as far as to say I felt great. I knew it was probably the adrenaline of looking out into the audience of over six hundred people patiently waiting for the music to start. At that moment, I didn't care why my sickness disappeared, I just needed it to stay away for twelve songs.

The first eight songs went off without a hitch, and we were playing as good as the four of us could sound together, but during the crowd banter before song number nine the sickness returned. I turned my back to the crowd and covered my mouth as I began to dry-heave. I then felt an impending vomit and forcefully swallowed it, leaving the taste of undigested Nyquil and Pedialyte in the back of my throat.

"Let's jump to the last two songs," I shouted to Travis.

"What?"

"I'm going to pass out or throw up all over your drum kit."

I then walked to the center of the stage and relayed the same message to Mark and Justin. Their reception of my impromptu set change was less than sympathetic.

"Are you fucking serious?" Mark asked.

"Sorry, I can barely stand, let alone play."

Mark glared at me and we began an old-fashioned standoff, but he quickly realized from my thousand-year stare that I wasn't budging. He spit onto the stage and walked back to the mic stand.

"I guess we are cutting the set short, so these are going to be our last two songs," Mark announced as he strummed his guitar.

A few weeks after the CD release we had a weekend tour booked in Lincoln and Des Moines, but the night before we were scheduled to leave Black Betty wouldn't start. Our options were limited to canceling the shows, renting a van, or asking another band if we could borrow theirs.

After a brief discussion, we decided we weren't going to cancel the shows and would drive two cars if necessary. We then began calling car rental companies and quickly discovered that renting a medium-sized van for the required four days would cost a minimum of $500. We didn't have that amount of cash, so that option was off the table.

Justin and Mark began calling members of different Denver bands in search of someone who had a van that met two requirements:

1. That was in proper working condition.

2. Was not being used that weekend.

After about an hour, we got lucky and found someone who would let us borrow their van in exchange for helping their brother move the following Saturday. I wasn't thrilled about spending a day off helping someone move, but we needed the van, so I grudgingly agreed to the deal.

Somewhere on I-80 around Gothenburg, Nebraska, I noticed the faint smell of gasoline. Within a mile, it had become unbearable. I became lightheaded and stuck my head out the window in an attempt to inhale fresh air.

"Did a fucking gas can tip over or something?" Mark asked.

"I don't know," I said, "but I'm getting high off the fumes!"

I pulled over on the shoulder and we executed a haphazard inspection of the van. Our search came up empty, and we concluded that one of the two gas tanks had a leak somewhere in the gas line and was emitting fumes into the interior of the van—and there was nothing we could do to fix it.

"Mark, you probably shouldn't smoke in here," I said as I merged back onto the highway.

"Good call."

We continued on to Lincoln and arrived at Knickerbockers that afternoon. We parked and exited the van as quickly as possible. The venue manager saw us standing outside the van and approached to greet us. He was about to shake my hand when he suddenly stopped.

"What the fuck is that smell? Are you guys huffing gas?" he asked.

"No, not today," I said.

He stared at me suspiciously for a few moments, probably contemplating whether he should let a bunch of gas-huffers into his venue. Finally, he half-nodded to the side door. "Load in over there."

Apart from the gasoline fiasco, the rest of the weekend was a close replica of our previous Midwest tours: playing music, hanging out with the locals, drinking to excess, passing out in the van, and driving across state lines on minimal sleep—cramming it all into a forty-eight hour period. Both shows had a larger crowd turnout than our previous stops in each city, and we were creating a Midwest fan base. I considered it a minor victory if the attendance increased each time we returned to a city that wasn't Denver, even if it was only a couple people.

I was driving on the return trip home, and barely awake. I had either become accustomed to inhaling gasoline fumes or the leak had stopped. The Denver Broncos and Oakland Raiders game was on an AM station, but I could hardly hear anything due to the poor reception. We were somewhere around Lexington, Nebraska when I heard an explosion that sounded like a shotgun. The van violently trembled between the dashed and solid highway lines, and it quickly became apparent that we had blown a tire.

There's something very terrifying about blowing a tire on a battered, old van with three other bald tires that is stacked ceiling-high with amps, drums, and other various music equipment—and doing it while traveling over 80 mph. The van was barely equipped to operate on four good tires at that rate of speed. With a flat tire I had visions of the van skidding into the gravel shoulder and rolling over and over until it reached its final resting stop in the Nebraska cornfields.

I don't remember exactly what I did next, but I think it was a combination of pressing on the brake and firmly gripping the steering wheel with both hands while maneuvering the van towards the right shoulder.

Once the van came to a complete stop I rested my head on the steering wheel and closed my eyes. My pulse was hovering around two hundred beats per minute.

"Holy fuck!" someone said.

"Fuck, I almost shit myself," I replied.

We exited the van and examined the rear right tire. It was disintegrated, smoking, and emitting a vile rubber odor. We began the process of changing the blown tire and immediately ran into a problem.

"Fuck, the bolts are rusted. I don't think we can get them off," Travis said as he dropped the four-way lug wrench onto the highway blacktop.

The four of us gave our best strong man effort, but the bolts didn't budge.

"Well, what are we supposed to do?" Mark asked.

"There's a town back there and maybe some sort of mechanic or auto store is open," I said, pointing back to the overpass.

I gave us a 50 percent chance the walk would be in vain. It was after 5:00 p.m. on a Sunday in October, and the odds of a tire shop or mechanic being open in whatever tiny town we came across weren't good. But we didn't have phone reception, so we didn't have another option.

Justin and I started the half-mile journey into oncoming traffic on the shoulder of I-80 headed toward exit 237. Semi-trucks sped by us a few feet from our path. It was deafening, and they jolted my entire body with each passing.

"These assholes don't give a fuck we're walking here!" I yelled as loud as I could.

"What?" Justin yelled back.

"Nothing!"

About thirty-five minutes later we arrived at a Super Wal-Mart that had an Auto Care Center, and to my surprise it was still open. We rushed to the back of the store and approached the auto counter, where a stereotypical Nebraska guy with a name tag that said "Bill" stood. His hands were in his pockets and he was chewing what looked like four pieces of gum.

"How can I help you fellas?" he said.

I quickly explained our situation.

"That sounds like a pickle, but I should be able to help you guys out," he said while blowing an oversized bubble.

"Really?" I said.

"I'll at least give it a try. Meet me outside, I'm going to grab a couple things."

Ten minutes later we pulled onto the shoulder behind the van in Bill's Ford F-150. He walked to the tire to investigate the predicament, probably thinking we were too incompetent to change a tire.

"Wow, those fuckers are on really good," he said after attempting to remove the lug nuts.

I watched as Bill walked to the F-150 and came back with a heavy-duty impact wrench attached to an air compressor in the bed of the truck. Within minutes the rusted bolts were removed and the disintegrated tire was replaced with the nearly bald spare.

"Thanks so much. We would have been fucked without you," I said as I handed him sixteen dollars, the amount of the collection I scrounged up from the rest of the band.

After the two-hour delay we were back on I-80 and speeding towards the Colorado border. The sun was setting fast across the horizon and we still had at least four hours until we reached Denver. The Broncos post-game show was on the AM radio station and the announcers were discussing their 59–14 massacre at the hands of the Raiders. I was in no mood for their jabbering so I turned the radio off then leaned back and started counting the mile markers like sheep.

I was about to doze off when I heard another explosion, then the van began to fishtail.

"Fuck, fuck!" Mark yelled as he attempted to correct the fishtail.

After a few tense moments he regained control of the van and began steering it into the median strip. I knew being parked in the median would put us at a higher risk of getting rear-ended by a sleep-deprived truck driver speeding in an eighteen-wheeler. I instinctively looked into the passenger-side mirror and, not seeing another vehicle pulled the steering wheel towards the right shoulder.

Less than two hours after blowing the rear right tire, we blew the front left tire. This time, however, we were in an even bigger predicament. The spare tire was already being used, and the van didn't have a spare for the spare.

It was 8:21 p.m. and we were over a mile from the closest exit and the town of Sterling, Colorado. I wasn't sure if that town had a tire shop, and I knew even if it did, it wouldn't be open at this hour on a Sunday night. I became anxious realizing that we might be fucked, but I was still hopeful that someone else would think of a way out of our predicament and a way home.

"We're really fucked," Travis said.

"Totally fucked!" Mark said as he jumped out of the van and lit up a cigarette.

We sat in the van for the next thirty-minutes brainstorming possible solutions. The results were futile, and I reluctantly conceded we were going to be spending the night on the gravel shoulder with semi-trucks passing us at uncomfortable distances.

"We could try AAA. I think if you sign up for the roadside assistance membership it comes with towing services," Justin said.

"Seriously?" I said.

"Yeah, I think you get a hundred miles of towing each year."

"And you don't have to wait to use it?" I asked.

"I don't know."

"How much is it?" Mark asked.

"I think a couple hundred bucks."

Justin spent the next twenty-minutes on the phone with a AAA representative working out the details while the rest of us hung onto every word. Finally, he looked up at us.

"There should be a tow truck here in about an hour."

We erupted into a celebration just as a semi-truck passed at a high rate of speed, producing a loud whooshing sound that shook the van. After the truck passed and the celebration ended, exhaustion set in and the van became silent as we waited for a tow truck to rescue us from the dark and desolate highway.

During the extended drive back to Denver I decided it was time to finally stop seeing Ana. She had been stringing me along since June with promises of separation and divorce, and it was making me an emotional wreck. I wasn't sure what her motive was. Maybe she really was planning on getting a divorce, maybe she was bored with her life and needed some excitement, maybe she wanted to sleep with a musician, or maybe she enjoyed having sex with multiple partners and marriage wasn't suited for her lifestyle.

On numerous occasions I had asked what she wanted out of our relationship. "I love you," she'd say, "and I want to be with you. But I'm married and need time to figure everything out." The more I heard that answer, the less I believed it.

I knew even if she did get a divorce, the odds of us being a couple were very, very slim. I had doubts that Ana would end her marriage and begin a relationship with the guy that broke up her marriage, and even if she did, she would probably resent me. I couldn't picture any scenario that would have us ending up together long-term, no matter how much I attempted to convince myself otherwise. It would never work out, I told myself, situations like this rarely do. The affair had an end date, and I wanted to end it on my terms, not Ana's.

But I had a rather significant issue. Somewhere along the way, I fell for her, and I fell hard. I was unsure if that feeling was truly reciprocated. She told me she loved me, but I pictured her telling her husband the same thing. I was upset at myself for falling for her, and I knew the longer I continued the affair, the worse I would get hurt. I knew I was going to be the odd person out, and the loser of the infidelity aftermath. It was going to be a no-win, lose-lose situation for me.

I planned on telling her we had to stop dating and I was going to start dating other people until she finalized her divorce. It seemed easy-enough and it should've been simply executed, but it wasn't. I skipped over one important step. I didn't tell Ana. I can't explain why. I think it was partly because I was scared, partly because I was weak, and partly because I was never good at confrontation. I just stopped talking to her.

For the first few days I succeeded and besides sporadic text messages our conversations were minimal. My texts were short with no future plans mentioned. The communication started to diminish and I was pleased with the results.

A few weeks after my decision I decided to get drinks with a girl named Beth. It was a lame attempt to forget about Ana. I did my best acting job to pretend I was enjoying myself, and after several Bud Lights and vodka shots Ana finally slid out of my consciousness and I began to enjoy myself. Being intoxicated is sometimes the easiest solution to the difficult problems.

I awoke the next morning lying next to Beth in her bed wearing only my boxers. My recollection of the night was blurry, but I had a strong hunch we slept together, or at least made a sloppy, drunken attempt at intercourse.

I began to feel guilty, and I was remorseful for what felt like cheating on Ana. It was a ridiculous notion, especially since I was the one that was single, but I couldn't shake the feeling. I was in love with a girl who was married and I just slept with a girl I didn't have any feelings for in an attempt to forget about the married girl. It didn't work, and I actually missed Ana more. I rolled out of Beth's bed, picked up my clothes, and exited the bedroom, quietly closing the door behind me.

About a month after I ended communication with Ana, we had a show booked at Moe's BBQ. I had initially invited Ana when we were speaking, but I also invited Beth sometime during our drunken evening together. I was hoping neither would attend.

Ana mentioned the show in a text message, but I immediately changed the subject. I never officially rescinded the invitation, but I thought from my lack of response she would take that as a hint that I didn't want her to attend, and the invitation had been withdrawn. Unfortunately, she hadn't picked up on this un-invitation.

I was standing onstage and warming up with "Longview" by Green Day when I glanced up and saw Ana walking into Moe's. I then looked over to Beth, who was drinking a beer at a table near the bar.

"Fuck, fuck, and major fuck!" I said as I took off my bass and leaned it against the railing.

Neither of them knew I had recently slept with each other, and it was my goal to keep it that way. I wasn't sure how I was going to interact with both of them without the other person getting jealous or suspicious.

I quickly walked to the table and sat next to Beth.

"Hey! How are you?" I asked.

"Good, you?"

"I have to take a piss, but other than that I'm good."

"Thanks for letting me know that."

"Sorry. Talk to you in a few?"

"Sure."

I jumped off the chair and intercepted Ana on her way to the bar.

"Hey! I wasn't sure if you were coming."

"Is it okay that I did?"

"Of course."

"Are you sure?"

"I invited you, didn't I?"

Ana nodded. Then we stood there, staring at each other. We didn't say a word, and it felt like we were strangers.

"Sorry to be so short, but I have to go to the bathroom then do soundcheck. Can we talk after we're done playing?"

"Of course. Have a good show."

I walked into the bathroom and looked at myself in the mirror. I watched droplets of sweat slowly transverse down my forehead like snails. I knew over the course of the next four hours I was going to have to have normal interactions with Ana and Beth while trying to keep them separated—and do all of this while becoming increasingly intoxicated. My blood pressure rose to a near anxiety attack-level just thinking about the rest of the evening. I thought about walking out the back door and not returning.

"Come on Scott, you can do this," I said, slapping my right cheek multiple times.

I spent the remainder of the evening pacing throughout the venue, not staying in one area for an extended period. I'd walk to the bar, then to the patio, then to the stage, then back to the bar, then to the bathroom, then back to the stage. When I did have a conversation with Ana or Beth, I'd excuse myself to the bathroom so frequently they must have thought I had a urinary tract infection.

I was exhausted before our set, and it showed. I played horribly. It was nerve-racking looking out into the audience and seeing Ana and Beth standing a few feet apart on the dance floor. The guilt got to the point that I considered announcing my apology to the entire audience: "Hey everyone, I am a fucking asshole and I deserve what happens to me."

We finished our set an hour later and I was packing my gear when Ana approached the stage.

"You guys sounded great."

"It wasn't our best night. I fucked up a bunch," I said as I looked up, smiled for a moment, then looked away.

It got quiet and neither of us knew what to say.

"Are you doing anything after this?" she finally asked.

"No. I think I'm just going to go home."

"Can I come over so we can talk?"

"Can we do it another night? I am exhausted," I said.

"Sure. Have a good night, Scott."

"You too Ana, drive safe."

She began to walk away, then stopped.

"I really miss you."

She resumed walking before I could respond, and I watched her until she disappeared out the front door. I had a feeling she wanted me to stop her, and I wanted to, but I was cemented to the stage, guilt-ridden.

The following day Mark and I were drinking at a local dive bar while watching college football and attempting to erase our hangovers from the previous night. At one point he turned away from the TV and squinted to enhance his vision of the parking lot.

"Isn't that Ana?" Mark asked, pointing to the sidewalk.

I instantly spun around on the barstool and leaned forward, almost losing my balance and falling to the tile floor in the process. At first I didn't see her due to the beer posters plastered on the windows, but then I saw her petite frame speeding toward the front door. She was walking with such swiftness that her feet were barely touching the sidewalk before she lunged into the next step.

"Fuck."

"Did you invite her?"

"No!" I said as I jumped off the stool and searched for an alternative exit.

"Well she looks pretty pissed."

"I can see that."

"I'd get the fuck out of here if I were you."

"That's my plan."

"Good luck man! I'll get your beers."

"Thanks," I said, without looking back.

I pulled my hoodie over my head in a poor attempt to disguise myself, and rushed to the front door with my head down focusing on the floor tiles. I was a few feet from the door when I saw feet that belonged to, I assumed, Ana. Then I felt a hand clutch my bicep.

"I need to talk to you."

"I'm not going to do this right now," I said as I pulled my arm out of her grasp.

"Bullshit, we're going to talk right now."

I finally looked at her, and I could tell she had been crying. And I knew she knew about Beth.

"I can't right now."

"Just tell me the fucking truth!" she shouted, drawing the attention of the patrons inside the bar.

I was about to respond when I noticed Ana was looking for something in her purse. I capitalized on the opportunity and slithered around her and out of the bar. As I jogged into the parking lot she followed my every step.

The game of cat and mouse continued for a few minutes until she finally caught up to me in a Chuck E. Cheese parking lot. She grabbed my arm again, this time with a stronger grasp, digging her nails into my skin. I was done running, and I decided it was as good a time as any to have our showdown.

"Please just tell me the truth," she pleaded, on the verge of tears.

"What do you want me to tell you?"

"Did you sleep with Beth?"

I paused, not knowing how to respond. I glanced towards the Chuck E. Cheese and saw kids playing video games and celebrating birthdays, and I could smell the aroma of cheap pizza.

"Please tell me. Is it true?"

"Yes."

Her lips began quivering and I looked at her then looked away. I wasn't strong enough to watch her cry. I looked at the passing light rail train, a nearby office building, and the for-lease sign in front of it, and then repeated the last four numbers in my head.

"Fuck you Scott! Fuck you!" she yelled.

That was the moment I realized she loved me, and the moment I realized I broke her heart.

She turned and walked away. I watched, and wanted to chase after her and tell her that I was sorry, but I knew it was pointless. I turned in the opposite direction and began walking back to the bar. I had walked about ten steps when I felt an enormous pressure on the back of my head, and then I felt it again. It took me a moment to realize that Ana had grabbed my hoodie and was punching me in the back of the head. Even with her small frame, the punches hurt. It felt like I was getting hit in the back of the head with a tennis ball.

She hit me three times and was in the process of the fourth swing, when I backpedaled out of her short reach to a safe distance. Her final swing only connected with air and resulted in her falling onto the pavement and landing on both palms and one knee. She remained there for some time, until her heavy panting eventually faded.

I was in shock, and it appeared that she felt the same. I think it's safe to say that she had never punched anyone in a Chuck E. Cheese parking lot. I didn't know what to do or say, and I waited for her next move.

"Fuck you, asshole!" she screamed with spit spewing from her mouth.

"What did you want me to do? We both know you aren't going to leave Josh!"

I had one armed extended to protect myself from another assault and the other hand checking the back of my head for any open cuts or gashes. She was trembling uncontrollably and I was unsure if she was going to cry, become silent, or make another combination attempt on my skull.

"I was planning on getting a divorce, and I just needed a little more time."

"Ana . . ."

"Goodbye Scott. I really did love you."

"Ana! Ana!"

She walked away and I watched as she quickly disappeared between two minivans. I looked up at the cartoon mouse giving me a thumbs-up then slowly lowered my head and began the long walk home.

For a few weeks I attempted to revive communications with Ana, but eventually I realized it was an exercise in futility. We had passed the point of no return and there was no going back. I not only fucked up the relationship, I fucked up our friendship.

A few weeks after our Chuck E. Cheese ordeal I saw a commercial for the DVD release of *Inception*. That was the only movie Ana and I saw in a movie theater, and the commercial was a reminder of all my missteps during the course of our relationship. I wondered if she thought about me when she saw the commercial, and I concluded that she probably didn't, and I knew I would never be able to watch *Inception* again without thinking of her.

Sometime around Thanksgiving I picked up my acoustic guitar and started strumming a riff I wrote years before, a song that never progressed beyond a musical verse. I repeated the riff for forty-minutes and then began scribbling down random lyrics in a notebook.

> *Now it feels like it's been forever since I've heard your voice, and I am scared that I'll forget what it sounds like.*

Three hours later I completed the music and lyrics. It only took a disastrous heartbreak to triumph over years of writer's block.

Highway to Hell
(Or Chapter 14)

December 2010 – June 2011

We played New Year's Eve at the Marquis Theater with three other Denver punk bands. It was a sold-out crowd of over four hundred people. We played second and were finished by 10:00 p.m., and I contemplated grabbing a cab and going home. I was still crestfallen about the Ana situation and was in no mood to be around people happily celebrating the New Year.

"I think I'm going to get the fuck out of here," I said to Mark.

"Fuck that, let's have a couple beers and go to the strip club."

Mark was in a similar relationship situation. He had married his long-term girlfriend the previous summer, but the marriage had begun to disintegrate. She had moved out of their house in the first week of December and they were preparing to sign divorce papers. Our lives were falling apart, and the only thing that was holding it together was the band and playing music.

I drank a beer with Mark, then another, and another, and before I knew it 2010 had concluded and 2011 had begun. I said goodbye to friends then walked outside and stood on the street corner attempting to hail a taxicab while holding my bass guitar case in the 10-degree weather.

The first few months of 2011 were bittersweet. Musically they were incredible, but personally they were a disaster.

The band was in the midst of its most successful stretch ever, and that allowed us to save up enough money to record our first full-length album, which was scheduled to be recorded in June and July of 2011. We were also in the process of scheduling our first California tour.

On the other hand, my personal life felt hopeless. I dated a few girls that winter, but each time I was reminded of how much I missed Ana. I either ended things after a few dates, or they ended them because they sensed I wasn't interested in them beyond an occasional hookup. I wasn't ready to date, and I'm sure I gave off the impression that I was a horrible person. I wasn't, I was just heartbroken. I'll admit the relationship with Ana was the definition of dysfunctional, but we were in love, and I fucked that up, and there was nothing I could do to fix it.

I considered moving away from Denver to get a fresh start, but I knew that required money and motivation, two things I didn't have. I did what I thought was the next best feasible solution: an *Eternal Sunshine of the Spotless Mind*-style exorcism in an attempt to erase Ana from my memory.

I deleted every text message, every picture, every email between us, I crumpled notes and letters and threw them in the trash, I deleted her as a friend on Facebook and I even threw away a T-shirt she gave me as a birthday present.

I sat on my couch and began to feel happy for the first time in months, until I realized I had written two songs about her and I'd be reminded of her every time I played a note from either song.

"Fuck!" I shouted to the ceiling.

"I don't care if you guys stay in here or come to the room, but if you do come to the room you better not make a fucking noise," Justin said as he slammed the van door.

It was sometime around 3:00 a.m. on May 21, and we were in a hotel casino parking lot somewhere in the middle of Iowa. Justin was upset that he had to drive through the night from Omaha to our hotel while Mark, Travis, and I continuously drank Keystone Light in the back of the van while being loud and obnoxious.

This was our fourth Midwest tour and fifth tour overall in under two years and tempers were becoming short. I didn't blame Justin for being upset, and I probably would have punched someone if I had to drive over four hours in the middle of the night through desolate sections of Nebraska and Iowa while the rest of the band was annoyingly drunk and requested me to pull over for a bathroom break every twenty-minutes.

Mark, Travis, and I remained silent. I didn't have to ask if we were going to stay in the van or go to the hotel room. It was a foregone conclusion. I watched Justin fade into the depths of the parking lot then turned around to Mark and Travis.

"How many beers are left?" I asked.

Mark reached into the twelve-pack box. "Six."

"Perfect, two each then we go inside and gamble."

The three of us sat inside the van in an Indian reservation casino parking lot drinking warm Keystone Light and watching headlights navigate the lot while listening to a mix CD that featured punk bands like Green Day, the Offspring, Sum 41, the Bouncing Souls, blink-182, Rise Against, Bad Religion, and Pennywise.

I was in a daze when Mark tapped me on the shoulder. "Let's go inside and grab a drink and play some cards."

We walked into the casino and surveyed the floor. The casino was practically empty, with the aroma of stale cigarette smoke from the previous night and the sounds of a vacuum cleaner in the distance. There was one blackjack table open. Two men sat at it playing cards with no conversation and little movement.

Mark and Travis walked to the blackjack table while I slogged over to the bar. I sat at the bar top and waited for the middle-aged bartender. I wanted to ask her if she knew the exact moment when her life took the wrong turn and led to working overnight shifts at a poor man's casino serving cheap beer and watered-down mixed drinks to degenerate gamblers who couldn't afford a plane ticket to Las Vegas. I decided pissing off the staff in the early dawn hours might result in an ass-kicking behind the casino and being thrown into a dumpster.

"Can I have a Bud Light?" I politely asked.

"No booze until six."

"Are you being serious?"

"Yes."

"Well what time is it?" I asked as I pulled my phone out of my pocket.

"A little after five."

"Fuck."

"Sorry. I can get you a soda or coffee if you'd like?"

"No. I'm good, thanks."

I rotated the stool away from the bar and debated joining Mark at the blackjack table with the gamblers looking for a pre-breakfast big score. I decided my lack of sleep and multiple hours of continuous booze intake probably would have resulted in adding incorrectly and me hitting on a hand of nine and a seven.

I saw a poster for the nightly cover band. I chuckled because on a few occasions I'd told Mark that when we were in our fifties we would probably move to Las Vegas and start a 1990s cover band that would play at some rundown casino off the Strip. Our sets would start at two in the morning and we'd play to a crowd that consisted of middle-aged, freshly divorced guys who were too drunk to locate their room or were drinking away their sorrows because they just lost their child-support money at the poker table. The older I got, the more I thought this had a possibility of becoming a reality.

I jumped off the stool, walked over to Mark, and sat next to him.

"No booze until six," I said.

My statement took a moment to register, but once it did he quickly took his eyes off the deck of cards to gauge if I was joking.

"Are you fucking serious?"

"Yeah. I'm going back to the van," I said as I walked away.

Mark grabbed his chips and jogged to catch up with me.

"Where's Travis?" he asked.

I shrugged. We searched the floor until we found him playing a penny slot machine. I explained the alcohol situation to him and we came to the consensus that we'd all return to the van.

Upon returning to the van the conversation was minimal, and I don't remember saying much of anything during that hour. It could have been that we were tired, or that we were drunk, or that we were each embracing life as a musician. The three of us sat in the van and watched the sunrise from a different perspective in a different state because we were touring musicians, and though we would return home with less money, we were pretending to live out our rockstar dreams, even if only at a minuscule level.

I awoke in the back of the van with potato chip crumbles and a half-eaten bag of Cool Ranch Dorritos in my lap. I looked around and noticed we were parked in a strip-mall parking lot. We were booked to play at the Bombay Bicycle Club in Des Moines that night, the third show of the tour, and we were the only band in the lineup and scheduled to play two sets. The venue was normally a dance club, and it wasn't accustomed to hosting a full band. Judging from the lack of stage equipment and the inexperienced sound guy, I wouldn't have been surprised if we were the first band to ever perform there.

Thirty seconds into our set the monitors stop working, then twenty seconds later the monitors began working again, this time accompanied by a high-pitched deafening sound that made it almost unbearable to perform, but we continued playing. The first song ended with little applause because almost half the audience, probably around fifty people, had either never stepped foot on the dance floor or had their back turned to the stage. I assumed they had arrived at the club expecting a DJ and a night of dancing and were pissed they had to listen to a punk band. The audience detested us, but we continued playing.

The fifth song was one we hadn't practiced or performed in months, and to put it in non-musical terms, we completely fucked it up. I forgot the verse, resulting in me playing incorrect bass notes through both verses, and Mark forgot the lyrics for a majority of the choruses, resulting in him repeating lines or just mumbling words in the key of the chorus. Luckily for us, almost no one was paying attention. We fucked up our own songs, but we continued playing.

The ninth song was where the train wreck of a set finally flew off the tracks. There was a power overload to the stage, causing the guitar amps, microphones, monitors, and the PA speakers to stop working, and the only noise that could be heard was Travis's drums. It was either a blown fuse or a disgruntled worker pulled a plug, but either way our first set had come to a disastrous conclusion. I figured it couldn't get any worse. I was wrong.

"I am going to get a few drinks and get really fucking drunk," I announced as I removed my bass and leaned it against my speaker cabinet.

I walked straight to the bar, attempting to avoid eye contact with everyone in the club.

"Can I get a Bud Light and a shot of Jäger?" I asked the bartender as I placed a twenty-dollar bill onto the bar top.

I was determined to be blacked out for the second set because I didn't want to have a recollection of the show. Travis came and sat in the stool next to me about ten minutes later, or in drinking terms, two beers and one shot.

"That was pretty bad huh?" he said.

"Probably the worst set I've ever played."

"Really?"

"If there was worse, I probably was too drunk to remember," I said, swaying back and forth. "Want to do a shot?"

"Yeah."

I motioned to the bartender then ordered a round of shots. We continued drinking and debated if we should play the second set or just throw in the towel. Travis heard an argument then abruptly turned back to the stage.

"Take a look at that," Travis said.

I slowly turned my head back toward the stage and saw Mark and Justin screaming at each other face-to-face. The PA speakers had resumed working so I couldn't hear what they were saying, but from their body language it seemed serious. If we planned to play a second set, a fight between guitar players was probably not an ideal way to start it.

191

In over a decade of knowing Mark I had never seen him remotely close to getting in an altercation, but from my vantage point on that barstool it looked like he was about to exchange blows with Justin.

"Should we do something?" Travis said.

"Nah, they're probably just pissed about how horrible we sounded. I'm sure they'll be fine," I said as I turned back towards the bar and ordered another beer.

A few minutes later Mark approached the bar and was trembling from the potential fight. He took a drink of my beer and said, "Fuck him. I'm done."

"What the fuck happened?"

"I told him to fuck off and that I was going to kill him."

"You said you were going to kill him?"

"I meant beat the shit out of him."

"So I take it we're not playing the second set?"

"Fuck no! I'm getting the fuck out of here."

"Where are you going?"

"I'm going to the airport and flying home," Mark said, starting toward the front door.

"Do you even know where the airport is?"

"No," said Mark.

Before I could respond he was gone and beyond shouting distance. I looked at Travis.

"Looks like we're finished for the night," I said.

"Looks that way."

A few minutes later Justin furiously approached the bar.

"Fuck that asshole! He can find his own ride home! He's not riding in the van with us!"

"I'm pretty sure he's sorry for whatever he said."

"He fucking threatened my life. He can go fuck himself," Justin said as he stormed away.

"What are we going to do about that?" asked Travis.

"I don't know," I paused. "Let's do another shot and hopefully I'll think of something."

I spent the rest of the night attempting to defuse the situation. I talked Mark out of getting a taxi to the airport, knowing the odds of getting a last-minute flight from Des Moines to Denver were close to zero, and even if there was one he didn't have the money to purchase a ticket. I asked him to apologize to Justin, but he refused.

Then I tried talking to Justin, but he was adamant about not letting Mark in the van for the return drive home. I finally gave up on my attempt to persuade both sides into apologizing and spent the rest of the night drinking at the bar. After last call I stumbled into the van, and passed out on the bench seat.

When I awoke the next morning the van was already heading west on I-80 towards Omaha. Justin was gripping the steering wheel and weaving in and out of traffic. There was no conversation and no music—the only sounds that could be heard were the large V-8 engine and the draft against the van. I leaned behind the seat and saw Mark sleeping on the floor.

Mark and Justin were in opposite sides of the van, as far apart as possible within the constraints of the space. Only about five feet separated them, but it might as well have been 500 feet. I knew they weren't going to say a word to each other, and that I was probably going to have to be the intermediary between the two.

I think we all understood that Justin was going to be kicked out of the band the moment we set foot on Colorado soil, and that created a high degree of tension. He was dead man walking. Replacing a rhythm guitar player was immensely easier than replacing a lead guitar player and lead singer who was also a charismatic front man. It was simple band math, and unfortunately for Justin, he would have to go.

The drive was like breaking up with your significant other on vacation, but still having to take the return flight home with them. I stared to the north and counted the wheat stalks passing by at 70 mph to kill time. It was moving at a snail's pace, and ten minutes felt like an hour. The drive seemed like it was never going to end.

After the longest drive of my life, we finally arrived back home and began unloading the van as quickly as possible. Ten minutes later the van was empty of Mark's, Travis's, and my equipment and luggage. Justin slammed the back doors shut, got into the driver's seat, and sped away into the night.

"Fuck, that sucked," I said.

"At least it's over," Mark responded.

He was right. The trip was over, but in some regards the band felt like it was also over. The four of us had practiced and performed together for over three years and it came to an unceremonious conclusion in a strip-mall bar in Des Moines, Iowa, over an argument that nobody really knew the origin of. We lost the band chemistry that night, and a band without chemistry is just noise.

American Idiot

(Or Chapter 15, aka the End)

July 2011 – March 2017

The band continued to play, sometimes as a three-piece, sometimes as a four-piece, but as the 2010s progressed practices fell by the wayside and shows became few and far between. With each passing year it became more difficult to sustain the dedication and motivation the band required. We grew up and grew older, and playing music didn't seem as important.

One winter evening in 2013 Mark and I were sitting on his couch drinking beers and watching a Colorado Avalanche game.

"I think it's time to call it quits," Mark said.

"The band?"

"Yeah. I think so."

"Fuck, I think you're probably right," I said, confident that our better days were behind us.

We booked our final show that March, almost five years since the day Mark and I sat on my couch and strummed the first chords of our first song. I never envisioned that drunken jam session would result in the most successful and gratifying musical experiences of my career.

We had a good run, in fact, I would call it a great run for a local band. We achieved success that most local bands could only dream of. Over the course of the band's lifespan we recorded one full-length album, two EPs, played hundreds of shows at countless venues in front of thousands of people, and shared the stage with some of our favorite bands.

"Thanks! It's been fucking amazing!" Mark said as the final note of our final song of our final show rang out.

Travis stood up from his drum throne and walked to the front of the stage and the three of us momentarily hugged then turned to the crowd of about 200 people and bowed one final time. I came close to tearing up on stage, but somehow I kept myself together. My adult life consisted of being a musician, and it was tough to grasp the fact that I may never walk onto a stage again.

About six months after our final show I was standing alone at the bar at an art exhibit waiting for the bartender when someone tapped me on the shoulder.

"Hello," I said as I turned around.

"You're Scott, right?" a girl asked.

"I am."

"I knew it was you! Your band is one of my boyfriend's favorite bands."

"My band?"

"Yes!"

"Are you sure?"

"Yes! He fucking loves you guys! Will you please come meet him and say hi? It'll make his night."

"Yeah, of course. Let me get a drink first."

"Here, take mine. It's a vodka soda."

She held out a plastic cup. I stared at it for a few moments then shrugged and reached for it.

"Where is he?"

"Follow me," she said as she grabbed my forearm.

We zigzagged through the crowd and past art pieces until she located her boyfriend.

"Steve! Look who I found at the bar," she said as we approached.

He stared at me blankly and I got the sense he had no clue who I was. I thought I was the victim of a practical joke. Then he turned to his girlfriend then back to me and smiled.

"I fucking love you guys!" he finally said.

"I heard. Thanks so much."

"I've always wanted to say thanks. Your songs got me through some rough times with an ex," he said, extending his arm for a handshake.

"I'm glad they helped," I said as I shook his hand.

"I'm Kurt, and this is my girlfriend Stacy."

"Hey guys, I'm Scott. It's nice to meet you."

"We actually met at one of your shows."

"That's really cool to hear."

"Almost three years ago," Stacy said.

"It is fucking awesome running into you here," he said.

"Likewise."

"Can I get you a drink or a shot?"

"Stacy already gave me hers," I said as I raised the plastic cup.

"Come find me when you finish that one. I want to buy you a drink."

"I will."

"Do you think you guys will ever play a reunion show?"

"Honestly, I don't know."

"Well if you do, we'll be there."

"Thanks. You guys have a good night."

I ran into Ana at a friend's wedding. It was on a beautiful summer evening that had a tranquil Colorado sky as a backdrop, a stark contrast to that bleak November night in the Chuck E. Cheese parking lot. It had been ten months since our falling out, and we had probably talked less than ten times since. I had accepted the fact that one day the text messages would stop and I would most likely never talk to her again.

She'd reconciled with her husband, and from everything I'd heard she was happy. I wasn't sure if she was truly happy or if she was faking it, but either way, I would never know the answer. I was definitely faking my happiness, and I'd convinced myself that I'd moved on and that I was over her, but I wasn't. I frequently thought about our final nights together and the different scenarios that could have played out, and what I could have said and done differently.

We sat on opposite sides of the aisle, and during the ceremony we made brief eye contact and smiled. I stared at her for what felt like an eternity, and then finally looked away before it got awkward. I had forgotten how beautiful she was, and it pained me seeing her sitting there in her black-and-white floral summer dress.

I don't know if it was the ceremony, or the booze, or just seeing her after a multiple-month-long hiatus, but I decided I was going to apologize for what happened between us. I knew this might be my last opportunity to do it face-to-face.

During the cocktail hour and dinner it didn't feel appropriate to initiate a serious conversation, and as I was finally getting up the courage I glanced up and saw her walking across the courtyard to the parking lot. I excused myself from the bar and jogged after her.

"Ana!" I yelled as I approached her car.

She looked up from her purse and turned back towards me.

"Are you leaving already?" I said out of breath, with one hand on the roof of the car to assist my balance.

"Yeah, I need to get home to the kiddo."

"Shit. I was kind of hoping we could talk. I have a few things I wanted to say to you."

"I don't know if that's a good idea."

"I understand," I said, then stopped for a brief pause. "I heard you guys are doing good."

"We are. Yourself?"

"I'm well. I'd say a seven out of ten."

"That's great. I'm happy for you."

"Thanks. Is it weird talking to me?"

"No, it's just different," she said.

"Yeah," I said as I looked away. "I miss talking to you."

"I really should get going."

"Well—I just wanted to say that I fucked up and I didn't realize how important you were to me until you were gone, and I am mad that we can't talk anymore or hang out. I'm sorry for everything that happened between us and I'm sorry the way it ended, and I'm just sorry."

"I'm sorry too."

We were silent for a few moments. I looked at the ground, then her, and then the ground again while she remained focused on her purse in the passenger seat.

"I wish we could go get a coffee or drink and catch up sometime," I finally said.

"You know that can't happen," she said, her voice dropping.

"So I guess this is goodbye?"

She rigidly turned away then fastened her seatbelt. I searched for something to say, but as I was about to speak I hesitated. There was nothing I could have said, and we both knew it.

Finally she turned back to me, and when she looked into my eyes, I knew that any fleeting hope I had of rekindling a relationship had ended.

"Take care, Scott."

"You too, Ana."

I backed away and she shut the door and started the car. I watched as she pulled out of the parking spot, then slowly drove across the gravel and turned onto the street and out of sight.

"I thought you guys broke up!" a drunk guy yelled to me on the Lost Lake patio.

"Fuck no. I'll probably be playing until I'm dead."

After a year-long hiatus I received a call from Mark. "Do you want to get the band back together and play a show?" he asked.

I pondered the question for about a total of four seconds before I responded, "Let's fucking do it."

Being away from music made me realize how much I loved playing and how much I took it for granted. It was my childhood dream to play in a band, and even though I didn't become a rockstar, I had one hell of a time doing it. I was aware that I had passed my musical expiration date, but I disregarded that asinine self-imposed restriction. I still had passion, talent, and the ability to prolong my dream—and I wasn't about to pass up an opportunity to play again.

I opened my bedroom closet and stared at the black gig bag leaning against the wall. My bass guitar had resided in that closet for nearly twelve months, played so infrequently that a pile of dust had accumulated on top of the bag. I blew off the dust and picked up the bag then placed it on my bed. I pulled the zipper down, opened the bag, removed the Stingray and flung it over my shoulder. I methodically began plucking the E string. From that moment, I promised to myself that I would cherish every performance, every practice, and every jam session, because each time could be the last.

We played our reunion show to a near-sold-out crowd, then another show a few months later, then another one and another one until we had accumulated about twenty post-breakup shows. We continued to get offered top-tier shows, so we continued to accept them.

Tonight's show was at a venue called Lost Lake. It was located in Denver on East Colfax and it was sandwiched between a nail salon and a liquor store. The venue was small with a capacity of about 200 people. The two exterior windows were plastered with countless stickers of bands that had played the stage and there was a yellow rectangular sign above the front door that simply read "Cocktails."

As I stood on the patio, an employee taped a piece of paper to the front door.

TONIGHT'S SHOW SOLD OUT

After all my years of playing, that phrase still produced an enormous smile.

"We go on in twenty-minutes," Mark said.

"Cool, I'll be in there in ten."

I excused myself from a group of friends and started walking west on Colfax Avenue towards the mountains.

When I reached the end of the block I stopped, then slid my hand into my pocket and pulled out a folded and withered piece of paper. I meticulously unfolded it and stared at the faded ink for a few moments under the illumination of a street light.

Music Checklist

~~Learn to play~~
~~Join a band~~
~~Play a show~~
~~Record an album~~
~~Go on tour~~
~~Play a show with a national band~~
~~Play a sold-out show~~
Get signed to a record label
Play Red Rocks

I looked up and watched the headlights of the oncoming traffic then turned around and started walking back towards Lost Lake.

"Seven out of nine isn't bad," I said as I tore up the paper.

"Master your instrument, master the music, and then forget all that bullshit and just play."
—Charlie Parker

CPSIA information can be obtained
at www.ICGtesting.com
Printed in the USA
FFHW011636040219
50418928-55593FF